The Secret of Power With God

by Dave Williams

D0980604

MOUNT HOPE BOOKS
A Division of Decapolis Publishing House
202 South Creyts Road □ Lansing, MI 48917-9284

Unless otherwise indicated, all Scripture quotations are taken from the *Authorized King James Version* of the Bible.

First Printing 1983
Second Printing 1993
Third Printing 2001

ISBN-938020-15-3

Published by Mount Hope Books
A Division of Decapolis Publishing House
202 South Creyts Road
Lansing, Michigan 48917-9284

Preface

The "secret" of power ...

The "secret" is really no secret at all for the person who understands the reality of Christ's power as found in the gospel accounts.

This book will show you how to tap the resources of unlimited power which could change the course of your life.

Jesus said, "The things which are impossible with men are possible with God" (Luke 18:27). In this book, you will study in a simple format, the keys to changing your prayer life into a power-packed time of accomplishing the impossible!

Let's move on now as we study the secret of *POWER WITH GOD*....

Table of Contents

1. Why Pray? 1
2. The Sin of Self-sufficiency 7
3. The Beginning of Power 13
4. Lord, Teach Us 19
5. "Habit" 21
6. Miracle of Thanksgiving 27
7. Prayer Management 31
8. What Power Is 35
9. Guidance From God 39
10. After Success, Then What? 45
11. When You Pray 49
12. "Our Father" 55
13. What Is God's Address? 61
14. God's Address, Part II 65
15. God's Address, Part III 69
16. God's Name and Holiness 71
17. The Coming World of Tomorrow 79
18. God's Will Or Some Other Will? 89
19. Three Steps to Discerning God's Will, Part I 93
20. Three Steps to Discerning God's Will, Part II 99
21. God's Interests 103
22. Principles of Petitionary Prayer 105
23. Forgiveness: Key to Power 113
24. Forgiveness — Continued 119
25. How to Forgive 123
26. Avoiding Evil 127
27. Christian Meditation 133
28. The Spiritual Language 139
29. Interpreting Your Spiritual Language 147
30. Obstacles 153

Why Pray? | 1 |

What is the secret of power with God? Why do some Christians seem to possess it while others do not? What is the key to breaking Satan's death-grip on this planet? I believe we can find the answers to these questions by taking a close look at Ephesians 6:10-18.

> [10] Finally, my brethren, be strong in the Lord, and in the power of his might.
> [11] Put on the whole armour of God, that ye may be able to stand against the wiles of the devil.
> [12] For we wrestle not against flesh and blood, but against principalities, against powers, against the rulers of the darkness of this world, against spiritual wickedness in high places.
> [13] Wherefore take unto you the whole armour of God, that ye may be able to withstand in the evil day, and having done all, to stand.
> [14] Stand therefore having your loins girt about with truth, and having on the breastplate of righteousness;
> [15] And your feet shod with the preparation of the gospel of peace;
> [16] Above all, taking the shield of faith, wherewith ye shall be able to quench all the fiery darts of the wicked.
> [17] And take the helmet of salvation, and the sword of the Spirit, which is the word of God:
> [18] Praying always with all prayer and supplication in the Spirit, and watching thereunto with all perseverance and supplication for all saints.

Verses 10 through 11 tell us that we must be strong in the Lord in order to stand against the tactics of our enemy, the devil. Verse 13 says we will be able to withstand the enemy if we put on the whole armor of God. And verses 14 through 17 gives us a piece-by-piece description of that armor.

Now, let's take a particularly close look at verse 18. It tells us to pray always with all prayer. That means "all kinds of prayer." PRAYER is the component that buckles on all the other parts of our Christian armor. Unless we make prayer a way of life, Satan is certain to introduce all kinds of complications into our lives.

Many people pray only when trouble arrives. However, many problems, difficulties, predicaments, embarrassing situations, temptations, and even tragedies could be avoided by making prayer a business — a way of life. Only praying believers can nullify and overthrow the evil designs and purposes of Satan. There is great turmoil in the world right now. We see the signposts on the road to Armageddon. It seems that Satan's last desperate onslaught against humanity has already begun. And there is one thing the devil is sure of: only praying Christians can break his death-grip on Planet Earth.

Satan knows that if believers fail to pray, they are vulnerable to his attacks. That's why he pours so much effort into diverting the Church from prayer.

WHY IS IT SO VITAL THAT WE GET ACTIVELY INVOLVED IN FAITH-FILLED PRAYER?

1. At this moment, the Church of Jesus Christ faces a historical opportunity that will not be repeated. Church leaders around the world sense a call of the Spirit to the ministry of prayer. If we don't act now by beginning ministries of prayer, both individually and corporately, we will be left behind when God brings His final end-time revival.

I believe there is a period of time, just in the future, when demon activity will reach its most fearful intensity. At this very moment Satan is busy at work, preparing and mobilizing his forces in anticipation of the coming Great Tribulation; the earth's final years of terror and bloodshed.

In this present, tense moment of history, the CHURCH holds the balance of power in world affairs, NOT the governments. You see, as long as God has His people here on earth, 2 Chronicles 7:14 is still in effect.

> If my people, which are called by my name, shall humble themselves, and pray and seek my face, and turn from their wicked ways; then will I hear from heaven, and will forgive their sin, and will heal their land.

2. God's plan from the beginning of Creation has been to work WITH man in governing the affairs of life and the concerns of this world! Prayer is sort of a PARTNERSHIP with God in carrying out His redemptive purposes in the earth.

> [18] Praying always with all prayer and supplication in the spirit, and watching thereunto with all perseverance and supplication for all saints;
> [19] And for me, that utterance may make known the mystery of the gospel,
> [20] For which I am an ambassador in bonds: that therein I may speak boldly, as I ought to speak. (Ephesians 6: 18-20)

Notice Paul requested prayer so that he'd be able to speak boldly and make known the mystery of the Gospel.

Let me share with you some quotes by some of the world's most renowned prayer warriors:

> God will do nothing but in answer to believing prayer.
> — John Wesley

> The greatest thing anyone can do for God and for man is to pray. Prayer is striking the winning blow ... service is gathering up the results.
> — S.D. Gordon

> God shapes the world by prayer. The more praying there is in the world, the better the world will be, the mightier the forces against evil... The prayers of God's saints are the capitol stock of heaven by which God carries on His great work upon the earth. God conditions the very life and prosperity of His cause on prayer .... Prayer should be the main business of the day.
> — E.M. Bounds

God wants us to work WITH Him in a partnership. And communication is a vital part of any partnership. Suppose your spouse never discussed matters concerning your family, your home, your finances, or any such thing with you? What kind of relationship would the two of you have? Not a good one, to say the least.

3. Prayerlessness is the NUMBER ONE cause of failure in Christian endeavors.

I know of a Christian businessman who owned a dying business until he learned the "secret" of communicating with God. Now his business prospers because of his "partnership" with God.

God desires us to have tangible results from our prayer life. Prayer is not to be without results. God encourages us to

4

expect great advantages through prayer.

The reason some people always seem to struggle through life is because of their slip-shod prayer lives. Have you ever heard people complain about never getting any "breaks" in life? Well, perhaps their lack of "golden opportunities" is a result of their lack of a "golden prayer time." Through prayer, day-by-day, we will begin to see God's plan unfold.

Do you want God's guidance in your life? Begin a regular time of Bible reading and prayer.

Andrew Murray said, "Without prayer, our witnessing and labor have little power." Is your ministry lacking power? Is your life lacking power? If so, check your prayer-power level. Faith-filled prayer is the secret of moving into the realm of the impossible. Faith-filled prayer is the key to moving heaven and earth for God. Success, whatever kind God gives to a person, depends on a consistent life of prayer.

What is the "secret" of power with God? The answer is so simple that most people overlook it all through life. The secret is **FAITH-FILLED PRAYER!**

The Sin of Self-sufficiency 2

"I can work things out myself!"

"Father, please! I'd rather do it myself!"

Does this sound familiar?

HUMANISM

Humanism is the belief that God is not needed. "Why do we need to trust God when we can put our faith in human potential?" That's humanism in a nutshell.

In recent history, we have listened to top evangelical leaders as they have stormed against humanism through television, magazines, books and other media. We've been made aware of this subtle adversary of God's plan.

What exactly is humanism? It is the recognition of man's claim to sovereignty and lordship. One humanist leader has said, "No deity will save us; we must save ourselves." The essence of humanism is not the denial of the existence of God, but the denial of His right to lordship over our lives.

Prayerlessness is actually a subtle form of humanism. It is the sin of self-sufficiency; the pride of independence. Genuine prayer has a means of dealing with this sophisticated sin.

SYMPTOMS OF THE SIN OF SELF-SUFFICIENCY

1. *A WRONG SET OF VALUES.*

[18] (For many walk, of whom I have told you often, and now tell you even weeping, that they are the enemies of the cross of Christ:
[19] Whose end is destruction, whose God is their belly, and whose glory is in their shame, who mind earthly things [Philippians 3:18-19]).

Instead of being authentically concerned about God's program and God's Kingdom, the person who harbors this sin will be only interested in the big "I," the big "ME." "What's in it for me?" "I-I-I-I-I." This person suffers from "I-trouble." He's willing to forget the Lord's Words and the Lord's work when it interferes with his personal or sensual desires.

2. *TOO MUCH EMPHASIS ON EARTHLY THINGS.* (verse 19)

This person lacks vision beyond what can be seen right now. He is only interested in the rewards and benefits here and now, with no mind for eternal things.

There is nothing wrong with earthly things. I enjoy my house and my car. I appreciate our beautiful and modern church facilities, but something is drastically wrong with the person who bases all of his decisions and actions upon earthy things instead of things having eternal and spiritual value.

3. *A FALSE SENSE OF MINISTRY.*

[21] Not every one that saith unto me, Lord, Lord, shall enter into the kingdom of heaven; but he that doeth the will of my Father which is in heaven.

²² Many will say to me in that day, Lord, Lord, have we not prophesied in thy name? and in thy name have cast out devils? and in thy name done many wonderful works?

²³ And then will I profess unto them, I never knew you: depart from me, ye that work iniquity. (Matthew 7:21-23)

Ministry to the Lord's people can never be a substitute for a personal, intimate relationship with Jesus. In fact, *NOTHING* can be a suitable substitute for prayer, *NOTHING!*

A false sense of ministry will get you doing things that are good in themselves, seemingly. But perhaps they are things that are not directed by the Lord. These fellows said, "Look what we did. We prophesied. We cast out devils. We did many wonderful things." But Jesus said, "Depart from Me, ye that work iniquity."

Because these "ministers" were busy with the "Lord's work," they figured everything was fine. But they failed in the most important area of life: to develop a close relationship with Jesus Christ and let the ministry flow from that relationship.

Effective and successful ministry and outreach are not the result of overwork — but of overflow — the overflow of Christ's life into ours as a result of intimate fellowship with Him.

Yokes are never broken, burdens are never lifted, and hurting people are never healed where there is no anointing from God. And that anointing from the Lord comes only through faith-filled prayer.

And it shall come to pass in that day, that his burden shall be taken away from off thy shoulder, and his yoke from off thy neck, and the yoke shall be destroyed because of the anointing. (Isaiah 10:27).

Why do some congregations have great joy and gladness while others do not? Why do some ministers see success while others do not? Why do some people face so many problems while others rise above their problems? The answer is faith-filled prayer.

Only anointed ministry is acceptable in God's sight. All labor for prestige, or for self-magnification or any other false motivation, is viewed by God as Babylonianism, or false religion. True ministry grows out of a vital, life-giving relationship with Jesus.

4. *A FALSE SENSE OF POWER.*

[15] I know thy works, that thou art neither cold nor hot: I would thou wert cold or hot.

[16] So then because thou art lukewarm, and neither cold nor hot, I will spew thee out of my mouth.

[17] Because thou sayest, I am rich, and increased with goods, and have need of nothing: and knowest not that thou art wretched, and miserable, and poor, and blind, and naked (Revelation 3:15-17).

These church members thought they had power because they were so financially stable. But Jesus saw them for what they were: wretched, miserable, poor, blind and naked. Perhaps they had worldly power, *but not the power with God.*

This church to whom Jesus addressed Himself believed that money alone was proof of their godliness. They had no needs, so why diligently seek the Lord? Why pray? They suffered from a false sense of power, a clear indication that

10

the sin of self-sufficiency had crept in.

HOW TO ELIMINATE THIS SIN

Authentic prayer will help eliminate this sin. The more you pray, the more you understand that apart from Jesus Christ, you can do nothing. At the same time a glorious balance is realized: apart from Christ you can do nothing, but through Him you can do all things.

> For without me ye can do nothing. (John 15:5)

> I can do all things through Christ which strengtheneth me. (Philippians 4:13)

The Beginning of Power | 3 |

What is the beginning of power with God? Where does it all begin?

Let me give you an illustration that will help you understand where the beginning of power with God rests.

For Christmas one year, my wife bought me a nice AM/FM radio with a built-in cassette tape player. Suppose I had never plugged it into a source of power. What would have happened? I'll tell you what would have happened. NOTHING! No matter how much I would have fiddled around with the switches and the knobs, nothing would have happened if I hadn't connected it to the power source.

In prayer, I can use all the correct rules and principles of praying, but if I'm not plugged into the Source of Power, my prayers are wasted. But how can I get plugged into the Source of Power?

Jesus said, "No man cometh unto the Father, but by Me." There is only one way to get plugged in to the true Source of Power, and that's to make your peace with Jesus Christ. How do you do that? Let's see:

1. *Acknowledge the fact that you're a sinner. Don't make any excuses.*

For all have sinned, and come short of the glory of God. (Romans 3:23)

And the publican, standing afar off, would not lift up so much as his eyes unto heaven, but smote upon his breast, saying, God be merciful to me a sinner. (Luke 18:13)

2. *You must see the awfulness of your sins and have a sincere desire to turn from them.*

I tell you, Nay: but, except ye repent, ye shall all likewise perish. (Luke 13:3)

Repent ye therefore, and be converted, that your sins may be blotted out, when the times of refreshing shall come from the presence of the Lord. (Acts 3:19)

3. *You must admit to God that you are a sinner and that you want to change.* Then tell somebody you believe that Jesus Christ rose from the dead and that He is really the Lord.

If we confess our sins, he is faithful and just to forgive us our sins, and to cleanse us from all unrighteousness. (1 John 1:9)

For with the heart man believeth unto righteousness; and with the mouth confession is made unto salvation. (Romans 10:10)

4. *But being sorry for your sins is not enough.* You must be willing to turn from them. You must want to be done with sin once and for all.

Let the wicked forsake his way, and the unrighteous man his thoughts: and let him return unto the Lord, and he will have mercy upon him: and to our God, for he will abundantly pardon. (Isaiah 55:7)

5. *You can't get rid of sin and evil by your own efforts.* The only way is to really believe in the finished work of Christ on the cross.

> For God so loved the world, that he gave his only begotten son, that whosoever believeth in him should not perish, but have everlasting life. (John 3:16)

> That if thou shalt confess with thy mouth the Lord Jesus, and shalt believe in thine heart that God hath raised him from the dead, thou shalt be saved. (Romans 10:9)

6. *You must personally receive Christ into your heart by faith if you expect to plug in to the real Source of Power!*

Right now, if you've never really asked Jesus to come into your heart, do it ... and He will.

> He came unto his own, and his own received him not. But as many as received him, to them gave he power to become the sons of God, even to them that believe on his name. (John 1:11-12)

Praying without a relationship with God is like trying to operate a radio with no power. It doesn't work. But when you come to Jesus Christ, you have the "connection" necessary to make your prayers full of power and authority.

So the first step to the beginning of power with God is a right relationship with God through Jesus Christ.

The second key to a power-packed prayer life is to GET QUIET.

> But thou, when thou prayest, enter into thy closet, and when thou hast shut thy door, pray to thy Father which is in secret; and thy Father which seeth in secret shall reward thee openly. (Matthew 6:6)

Be still, and know that I am God. (Psalm 46:10)

Study to be quiet. (Thessalonians 4:11)

Personal quietness is not something that is natural. It must be learned. Most of us talk too much and listen too little.

A certain minister had a parishioner who called him frequently. She would air all of her grievances and problems, and talk incessantly about things of no value at all. She wouldn't even let the minister get a word in edgewise. He quickly began to dread her calls.

One day he was praying, "Oh Lord, please don't let that woman call me today. All she does is gibber-jabber, and I can't get a single word into the conversation!"

Suddenly, at that moment, the Lord spoke to his heart and said, "That's what you've been doing to Me for years!" Of course this shocked the preacher because he was so used to only talking *to* God in prayer. It had never occurred to him to listen. But that single incident changed his prayer life. Now he not only talks to God, but listens to God.

Many Christians say, "Listen up, Lord. Your servant is speaking." But the Christian who has learned the secret of power with God says, "Speak, Lord. Your servant is listening."

Jesus said to go into the closet and shut the door. In other words, go somewhere you can shut the door to the cares and problems of life. Go somewhere you won't be interrupted; go to a secret place. Go somewhere you can be alone with God.

Learn the amazing secret of getting quiet before the Lord. God refuses to shout over the noise of the world.

So the second secret to power-packed prayer is to learn the art of personal quietness. Get alone with God each day in a "secret" place.

THE PRESENCE OF GOD

The third secret of power-packed prayer is to focus on God's presence. He has promised to never leave you nor forsake you. He has promised to be with you until the end of the world.

There is another world watching you. God is in the room with you right now.

Prayers need not be shouted so heaven can hear them. God is in your room — right there now!

Jesus taught that true worshippers would not only worship in the Temple or in the mountain, but everywhere! He said, *"in Spirit and in truth"* (John 4:21-23).

Moses was so conscious of the need of God's presence, he said he wouldn't go anywhere without God's presence going also.

> And he said unto him, If thy presence go not with me, carry us not up hence. (Exodus 33:15)

Three teenage girls were in a rowboat that had drifted far from their parents' cottage. It was getting dark and they became frightened. They screamed, they hollered, they frantically called for someone to help them, but their cries were not heard and help did not come.

One of the girls remembered the truth that God is everywhere. She quoted a Scripture verse that Jesus spoke concerning His nearness. The three girls decided to quit yelling, get quiet, and focus upon the presence of God instead of their dilemma. They prayed and rejoiced in Jesus and within a matter of minutes they were rescued.

Focusing on God will do two things:

1. Our prayers will become positive instead of negative.

2. We can pray without becoming discouraged because we are no longer depending upon ourselves, but upon God!

Do you want to participate in the power of God? Take thirty minutes a day to get quiet and relaxed before the Lord. Recognize His presence. Talk with Him and listen to Him. He'll help you plan your day. He'll give you ideas. He'll change your life!

Lord, Teach Us | **4**

One of the keys to success, whatever the endeavor may be, is to learn from the experts. Do you want to be a successful singer? Study the lives of experienced, successful singers. Do you want to be used of God? Make yourself a student of men and women who are being used of the Lord.

The same principle holds true in prayer. If you want to learn how to be an effective, successful pray-ER, study the life of an effective, successful pray-ER.

In this chapter we will look into the human side of the Greatest Pray-ER that ever lived. He was divine, but He was also very much human. His anointing came not because of His divinity, but as a result of His life of prayer, as we shall see. Who is this powerful Person of prayer? His name is JESUS!

Let's look at Luke 11:1:

> And it came to pass, that, as he was praying in a certain place, when he ceased, one of his disciples said unto him, Lord teach us to pray, as John also taught his disciples.

LORD, TEACH US

This Scripture reference doesn't tell us which disciple asked the Lord to teach them to pray, but whoever he was, he certainly understood the success principle previously mentioned. He sought to learn from the Great Expert Himself.

He didn't call upon the Pharisees, the modern day religious leaders, to teach him how to pray. You see, the Pharisees' prayer-life was dull, dry, cold, and lacked real power. Why should he ask a "failure" how to be successful? But look who the disciple did ask! He called upon Jesus, a man who didn't seem to have a religious bone in His body. Though He was the eternal Son of God — God Incarnate — He seemed so ordinary, so common, yet there was something about His prayer-life that caused this disciple to want to learn more about prayer.

To the Pharisees, prayer was only a *form*, consequently, a farce! But to Jesus, prayer was not a farce, but a MIGHTY FORCE!

The disciples saw something in Jesus' prayer-life they wanted. They saw results. They, too, desired their lives to experience that same anointing of power.

You can experience power with God as you put into practice the prayer principles taught in this book. You can change your prayer-life from a form to a FORCE.

In the following chapters we'll take a closer look at the prayer-life of our Lord.

We are now going to peek into the earthly life of our Lord to see if we can learn some important "secrets" of power with God.

PRAYER WAS A WAY OF LIFE WITH JESUS!

> But Jesus often withdrew to lonely places and prayed. (Luke 5:16 NIV)

Prayer was not merely a "fire escape" or a "spare tire" with Jesus; it was a habit, a way of life with Him.

A habit is like a cable. We weave one thread at a time. The more threads we weave, the stronger the cable becomes. The more we pray in faith, on a daily consistent basis, the more powerful our prayers will become.

There is something better than "getting prayed up," and that's "staying prayed up." Can you imagine a demon-possessed man coming to Jesus for deliverance and Jesus looking at him, saying, "I have to go get prayed up first!" No sir! Jesus *stayed* prayed up. That's a key to real power with God.

RESULTS OF BEING "PRAYED UP"

Power flowed from Jesus after spending a regular time in prayer.

> [16] And he withdrew himself into the wilderness, and prayed.
>
> [17] And it came to pass on a certain day, as he was teaching, that there were Pharisees and doctors of the law sitting by, which were come out of every town of Galilee, and Judaea, and Jerusalem: and the power of the Lord was present to heal them (Luke 5:16-17).
>
> [12] And it came to pass in those days, that he went out into a mountain to pray, and continued all night in prayer to God.
>
> [17] And he came down with them, and stood in the plain, and the company of his disciples, and a great multitude of people out of all Judaea and Jerusalem, and from the sea coast of Tyre and Sidon which came to hear him, and to be healed of their diseases;
>
> [18] And they that were vexed with unclean spirits: and they were healed.
>
> [19] And the whole multitude sought to touch him: for there went virtue out of him, and healed them all (Luke 6:12, 17-19).

EARLY CHURCH

The early disciples set a special daily hour of prayer, in following Jesus' example. The results? **POWER** flowed from them.

Stephen, an ordinary lay person, a member of the church, began to do wonders and miracles among the people (Acts 6).

Philip, another lay person, began to preach and cast out devils. Power flowed from him, the sick were healed, and miracles occurred (Acts 8)!

And look at Acts 5:14-16:

¹⁴ And believers were the more added to the Lord, multitudes both of men and women.

¹⁵ Insomuch that they brought forth the sick into the streets, and laid them on beds and couches, that at the least the shadow of Peter passing by might overshadow some of them.

¹⁶ There came also a multitude out of the cities round about unto Jerusalem, bringing sick folks, and them which were vexed with unclean spirits: and they were healed every one.

MIRACLE SERVICE

We conducted a miracle service in our facilities a few months ago. The power of God was present to heal. Many testimony reports came into our office afterwards. "Cancer healed!" "Arthritis gone!" "Multiple Sclerosis disappeared!" Healings and marvelous miracles occurred and greatest of all, scores of people gave their hearts to Jesus at the close of our service.

One young professing atheist walked into the building that morning and said there was something like "electricity" all over the place. There was a strange sense of **POWER** in the air. At the end of the service, he came forward to receive Jesus Christ.

I lifted my hand to pray for a lady and when I did she fell over backwards. She got up, so I lifted my hand again to pray, and the power of God encompassed her again and down she went for a second time!

My associate and I were both praying for the sick. Hundreds were forcibly overcome by the power of God and fell over backwards ever-so-gently! One lady, an intelligent, reasonable person (not a fanatic) testified concerning a vision she experienced while "under the power of God."

Scores of lives were healed and miraculously changed that day by the power that was present to heal. (Luke 5:17)

Where did this power originate? It originated with God and was transferred to us by the Holy Spirit as we invested time with Him in prayer. Our whole church invested seven days in faith-filled prayer prior to that one "miracle service." We fasted, we prayed, we "fine-tuned" our faith, and God gave the desired results.

The reason many people, even church leaders, don't display a greater anointing of power is because they are lazy or haphazard in their prayer-life. They're not willing to spend quality time with God on a daily, consistent basis in prayer and in the Word.

CHANGE YOUR LOOKS!

Another interesting fact about developing a regular, consistent habit of daily prayer is that your countenance can actually be changed!

It happened to Moses. (Exodus 34:29-35)

It happened to Jesus:

> And as he prayed, the fashion of his countenance was altered, and his raiment was white and glistening. (Luke 9:29)

A powerful man of prayer spoke at our church and related to us an incident which happened at Chicago's O'Hare Airport. He was making his way through a crowd and noticed a man going the other direction. There was something about the man's countenance that Judson instinctively *knew* was the look of a genuine worshipper. So he turned around, ran after the man, finally caught him, hugged him and said, "Praise the Lord! It's so wonderful to meet a real worshipper at this airport!" Sure enough, it was true, the man was a born-again person of prayer and worship!

If you are a man or woman who has a daily, consistent time of prayer, it doesn't take you very long to find out who is really giving themselves to prayer and who is NOT. You can actually tell by their countenance.

When I met the girl who would later become my wife, I knew there was something powerful and wonderful about her. She radiated. There was something that flowed from her countenance. At the time, I was pretty young in the Lord and didn't know what it was. Later I found out that she was daily going to the golf course in the early hours of the morning before the golfers arrived, and there she was praying and worshipping the Lord.

A habitual, daily hour of prayer will give you a new power, a new anointing, and even a new look!

Miracle of Thanksgiving | 6 |

We are continuing to study the exciting, powerful prayer life of our Lord Jesus. First, we learned that prayer was a habit — a way of life — with Him. Let's look now into a second important aspect in Jesus' life of prayer.

JESUS WAS A THANKFUL PRAY-ER

Father, I thank thee that thou hast heard me. (John 11:41)

And he commanded the people to sit down on the ground: and he took the seven loaves, and gave thanks, and brake, and gave to his disciples to set before them; and they did set them before the people. (Mark 8:6)

At that time Jesus answered and said, I thank thee, O Father, Lord of heaven and earth, because thou hast hid these things from the wise and prudent, and hast revealed them unto babes. (Matthew 11:25)

Jesus didn't concentrate on problems, troubles, difficulties, or "impossibilities." He entered prayer with thanksgiving in His heart and thanksgiving upon His lips.

The reason many people are unsuccessful in their prayer warfare is because they enter into prayer with heaviness, gloom, complaining and griping. Psalm 100:4 exhorts us to:

Enter into his gates with thanksgiving, and into his courts with praise: be THANKFUL unto him, and bless his name.

TO BE THANKFUL IS TO BE PRODUCTIVE

Years ago I had a friend who was a new believer. He was hungry for more of God's Word, so I took the time to copy some Bible teaching tapes for him. We didn't have a high-speed duplicator, so it took a considerable amount of time to copy even one tape. But I did it for him because I felt he needed some good, solid Bible teaching. There were no full-gospel churches in his city.

After I gave him the copied sermon tapes, he said, "Oh thanks so much, Brother Dave. I can't tell you how much I appreciate this. Thanks!" He showed such a sincere appreciation for what I had done, that I actually felt like a king! It made me feel terrific that this guy was so thankful and appreciative.

After that, I found myself joyfully making more tapes for the brother. It was a real joy doing it because he genuinely appreciated it. By being thankful, this guy's tape library multiplied.

God taught me an important principle through this experience. He spoke to my heart and said, *"I ENJOY giving good gifts unto My children who appreciate Me. No good thing will I withhold from them that are thankful (which is an element of walking uprightly)."* (See Matthew 7:11 and Psalm 84:11.)

Look at what God's Word says about thanksgiving:

1. Promise of deliverance to the thankful. (Psalm 50:14-15)
2. Loaves and fishes multiplied after Jesus gave thanks.

28

(Mark 8:6-9)
3. Our requests to God are to be made with thanksgiving (Philippians 4:6).
4. We should thank God because He is good (Ezra 3:11).

LADY HEALED OF CANCER

I was the guest speaker at a city-wide Thanksgiving service. I spoke on the value of giving thanks, even when everything looks bad. I called it "The Miracle of Thanksgiving."

A certain pastor's wife was in that service who recently had been diagnosed as having cancer. She was gloomy and depressed, but after learning about the "Miracle of Thanksgiving," she enthusiastically went home and began to thank the Lord for the many good things He had done in her life. She quit complaining about her cancer and started thanking the Lord for her family, her home, everything she could think of.

Well, I guess you know the rest of the story. Her health began to improve. She went back to her doctor and he called it "A Miracle." The cancer had disappeared!

ATTITUDES

There are two kinds of attitudes: Victory or Failure. A victory attitude is full of thanksgiving. A failure attitude is full of complaining and grumbling. One of the chief sins of the children of Israel was their failure to be thankful. Instead, they grumbled which led to their destruction.

> And do not grumble, as some of them did and were killed by the destroying angel. (I Corinthians 10:10 NIV)

One of the quickest ways to get your spirit overwhelmed with gloominess is to begin complaining. Conversely, one of the greatest ways to get your eyes off the bad circumstances and onto the miracle working power of Jesus Christ is to count your blessings and begin thanking God for all the good in your life.

> I complained, and my spirit was overwhelmed. Selah.
> (Psalm 77:3b)

You can't enjoy a watermelon if you keep complaining about the seeds. In the same way, you can't enjoy life if you keep complaining about the few "seeds."

Do you want to know how to experience power with God? Learn from Jesus. Enter prayer with thanksgiving and praise. Thank God for even the little things: the carpeting, the oil in the car, the refrigerator, your socks, everything!

Prayer Management | 7

What priority do you place upon prayer? Does it hold a position above education, attitude, determination, and hard work? Or is it a notch lower on your priority scale?

Education is important. A healthy, positive attitude is basic to success and victory. Determination is a stage of genuine faith, and hard work is essential to all high-level achievement. But as wonderful as these ingredients are, they were never meant to be a substitute for prayer. They are supplements to prayer, but not substitutes. There are no adequate substitutes for consistent personal prayer.

Jesus knew this! And He never substituted anything for His personal prayer-life; not ministry, not work, not anything!

JESUS NEVER SUBSTITUTED WORK
OR MINISTRY FOR HIS PERSONAL PRAYER LIFE

[15] But so much the more went there a fame abroad of him: and great multitudes came together to hear, and to be healed by him of their infirmities.
[16] And he withdrew himself into the wilderness, and prayed. (Luke 5:15-16)

The crowds were pressing Jesus for more healing and more ministry. But Jesus felt the urgent need to withdraw and pray. He knew that His ministry to others, as important as it was, could never, even for a day, be a replacement to His personal time for prayer.

WISE OLD MINISTER

While on a speaking assignment at a conference, an internationally known minister was approached by another Christian minister whose morale seemed to be at an all time low.

"I don't know what's wrong," the young minister groaned. "I work from seven o'clock in the morning until nine o'clock every night and I just seem to be going in circles. I'm so frustrated in the ministry. I just can't seem to...."

"Excuse me for just one moment," interrupted the wise older minister. "How much time are you spending in daily prayer?"

"In what?"

"In daily, consistent prayer. How much time are you spending in it?"

"Oh Uhm, Ah....Well, ah, not very much, I guess."

So the old preacher had the problem pinpointed and was able to help the young minister set up a schedule of priorities. Oh yes, there were some things on the agenda that had to be deleted (as "impossible" as that seemed), but it was worth it. Before long, the young man's ministry became increasingly productive and more and more fruitful. He was even finding time to enjoy his family (which is vital to any genuinely successful work).

PRAYER MANAGEMENT

Poor prayer management is one of those behind-the-scenes problems that generally surface after the damage has already been done. Don't make the tragic mistake of trying to substitute hard work for prayer. Even seemingly good things, like ministering to others, can never be a suitable replacement for regular personal contact with the Father.

Do you want your life to be less frantic and more productive? If so ... **PRAY!**

What Power Is | 8

We are studying the SECRET OF POWER WITH GOD. What is "power" anyway? Power is defined as "the ability or capacity to act or perform effectively." Power is:

- strength
- authority
- energy
- influence
- greatness

When you lose power, you lose the ability to perform effectively. You lose strength, authority, energy, influence, and greatness. Without power from God, the believer's life will gravitate into mediocrity and lukewarmness. Losing power with God is disastrous.

A few years ago, a passenger jetliner plunged into the frozen Potomac River, sending 78 people into eternity. At the time, authorities didn't understand what caused that Boeing 737 to crash. They thought that for some reason there wasn't sufficient power for the plane to maintain altitude. They thought the engine power had weakened enough to cause the law of gravity to overtake the law of lift and consequently, a tragedy occurred!

And tragedy will occur in the believer's life if he loses power with God. Doors will close, opportunities will be thwarted, plans frustrated, ever increasing disappointments and discouragements will appear, and eventually the believer's testimony and ministry will be neutralized. All this is a result of losing substantial power by reason of a prayer deficiency!

One of the chief causes of a prayer shortage in one's life is the feeling that God is not listening. Haven't you ever *felt* as though your prayers have not left the room?

Well, in the prayer-life of Jesus, we find Him always praying with full confidence that the Father heard Him.

JESUS ALWAYS PRAYED WITH FULL CONFIDENCE THAT THE FATHER HEARD HIM

> [41] Then they took away the stone from the place where the dead was laid, And Jesus lifted up his eyes, and said, Father, I thank thee that thou hast heard me.
> [42] And I knew that thou hearest me always: but because of the people which stand by I said it, that they may believe that thou hast sent me. (John 11:41-42)

As believers, we too can go to God in prayer with FULL CONFIDENCE that He hears us. We may not always *feel* as though our prayers are being heard, but they are! God is not a liar.

> Call unto me, and I will answer thee... (Jeremiah 33:3)

> [14] And we are sure of this, that he will listen to us whenever we ask him for anything in line with his will. [15] And if we really know he is listening when we talk to him and make our requests, then we can be sure that he will answer us. (1 John 5:14-15 TLB)

God hears us, not because we feel like He hears us. Nor does He hear us because we are so good. He hears us because when we pray, we do it all in the righteousness and Name of our Lord Jesus! When God sees us, He sees us through His Son, therefore He doesn't see our "royal nastiness." He sees only His beautiful children, cleansed by the Blood of Jesus Christ, and made spotless by faith in that Blood.

Isn't that wonderful? That means that God perks up His ears just as quickly for you as He does for any of the top Christian leaders in the world today!

God is just looking for ways to give good things unto His children.

> If ye then, being evil, know how to give good gifts unto your children, how much more shall your Father which is in heaven give good things to them that ask him? (Matthew 7:11)

But notice the requirement! It's not that you do a certain number of good deeds. It's not that you wait for a special feeling. The requirement is that you ASK! That's it!

> Ye have not, because ye ask not. (James 4:2)

> ASK, and it shall be given you. (Matthew 7:7)

> And all things whatsoever ye shall ASK in prayer, believing, ye shall receive. (Matthew 21:22)

> [13] And whatsoever ye shall ASK in my name, that will I do, that the Father may be glorified in the Son.
> [14] If he shall ASK anything in my name I will do it! (John 14:13-14).

Read these Scriptures daily. You will find your confidence expanding and snowballing. Remember, our faith in

God cannot be predicated upon our feelings, our emotions, or our so called righteousness. Sometimes we "feel" as though God is not listening, but if you have made Jesus Christ your Savior and Lord, God is listening regardless of how far away you may feel He is at times.

Jesus prayed with full assurance that the Father heard Him. You can too! Just *ASK*! God hears you and will answer. He has promised!

Guidance From God | 9

Life could be so simple! It could be so uncomplicated if we'd only learn there are only two roads we can travel. There's the "road of God's will," and there's "some other road." No matter what the "other road" may be, it's the road to failure.

JESUS SPENT EXTRA TIME IN PRAYER
WHEN FACING IMPORTANT DECISIONS

Jesus understood the great importance of finding the Father's "road" for Him to travel. He realized that God's will was the only path to success. So guidance from the Father was paramount in Jesus' life and ministry. In fact, He spent the entire night in prayer before asking anyone to join His apostolic ministering team.

> [12] And it came to pass in those days, that he went out into a mountain to pray, and continued all night in prayer to God.
> [13] And when it was day, he called unto him his disciples: and of them he chose twelve, whom also he named apostles. (Luke 6:12-13)

It's easy to let the "voice of logic" or the "voice of inclination" interfere with God's voice. But that's the road to ruin!

I know people who have joined religious cults because they had "a witness in their hearts" that it was the true religion.

Jimmy Kempner, a former Mormon, now a Christian minister, visited the Mormon temple in Salt Lake City, Utah. There he talked with several young people who were awe-stricken at the elaborate and magnificent architecture of that building. As these young people testified, they said that as they stood before the statue of Jesus at the Temple, God "witnessed to their hearts" that Mormonism is the only true religion.

That's what I call the "voice of inclination." Satan is clever at giving "a witness" in your heart. A careful study of Mormonism would reveal that it is one of the foremost religious cults in the world today. Yet these young people had a "witness" in their hearts, as they called it.

To let the "voice of inclination" override the "voice of God," is one mistake that leads to destruction and utter shipwreck.

LOGIC

Then there is the "voice of logic." That voice also invariably tries to usurp the authority of God's voice.

Let's see! The "voice of logic" would have told Jesus to choose some important people for His apostolic team. For example:

- A banker — Just in case the ministry gets in financial difficulty.

- A lawyer — To get the Jesus Christ Evangelistic Association out of trouble when the government started investigating their tax-exempt status.

• A book publisher — To get Jesus' words recorded and onto all the newsstands in the country.

Of course I'm being facetious, but I'm trying to illustrate a truth. There is nothing wrong with having a banker, a lawyer, or a book publisher on your staff ... *IF* God directs you to choose them. But if you appoint them because it's "the logical thing to do," irrespective of what God's thoughts are, you are heading for trouble.

Look who Jesus chose after praying all night: a tax collector, some fishermen, and a few other "unknowns" including a thief! And though one disciple fell away from Jesus, the other eleven turned the world right-side-up!

Jesus listened to the voice of His Father more than the voice of logic.

Do you want to be successful? Then follow the example of Jesus. Spend enough time in prayer until you have an absolute assurance — a *KNOWING* — of God's will and direction. Never make a major decision, regardless of the pressure, without seeking the mind of God.

Don't be just a casual inquirer! Pray things through until assurance comes! If your heart needs to be dealt with, God is big enough to do it if you'll just spend time with Him. Ask for guidance from your Bible and from an inner "*KNOWING*."

STUPID THING!

I did a stupid thing several years ago. I was a new minister with great enthusiasm and a "message for the world," I thought. But I didn't know how to obtain ministering assignments in the churches ... so I trusted my logic! I figured if I could put together some good promotional material and send it to all the churches, they'd respond by begging me to come and speak to them from their pulpits. What pride!

Well without praying the matter through, I designed a colorful advertising packet and sent it to churches all over. I waited a couple of days with great anticipation, then searched the mailbox. Nothing. I waited a week. Then a month. That was several years ago and I still haven't heard from those churches! (Praise God! I hope they forgot about me.)

So I began to seek the Lord like never before. I promised Him I would never again ask any human being for a place to preach. I would seek Him and Him only. As I prayed, studied, and waited upon the Lord, a new assurance and confidence began to rise up in my heart.

Then one morning as I was talking with the Lord, a "KNOWING" came to my heart; an indescribable assurance came to me that a certain influential pastor was going to ask me to speak and after I did, a whole new era of ministry for my life would open. I ran upstairs and told my wife, "Guess who's going to ask me to preach?" She asked, "Who?" So I told her about this amazing assurance that came to my heart — this supernatural "KNOWING."

A couple of weeks passed by and it happened! One of the leading pastors called and asked me to preach. "I already have my message prepared!" I told him.

That was the beginning of a whole new phase of ministry for me. And I've been busy ever since!

Thank God I learned that logic can lie, but God cannot. A "witness in your heart" can lie, but God's assurance cannot. Why take a chance on logic or an unsure "witness" when you can have God's perfect guidance and direction? That's the road to *real* success.

"Your key to power with God for today: On important issues and decisions, pray until you have God's assurance and a supernatural "KNOWING" of the right course to take. Logic is good, as far as it goes. And sometimes God will give you an inner witness, but pray until you are sure the "witness" is from God, and not just your own inclination.

After Success, Then What? 10

After success comes, then what? After your prayer has been answered, what next? Is it possible to grow beyond the need to pray? Can we reach a spiritual maturity where prayer is no longer necessary? Why pray if you have no needs?

Let's continue to look at the prayer-life of Jesus. Let's see what Jesus did at the peak of His popularity.

> And when he had sent the multitudes away, he went up into a mountain apart to pray: and when the evening was come, he was there alone. (Matthew 14:23)

Jesus had just dismissed multitudes of people that had attended His meetings. There were probably 10,000 people including the women and children. That's enough people to fill a good size arena or stadium. So Jesus was a popular figure, to say the least.

It is at this point — the height of success — that many quit praying, or at least begin to slack off on their prayer-life. They start to trust in the momentum to keep them going. They've gained popularity, fame, success! "Nothing" they begin to think subconsciously, if not consciously, "can stop me now!"

But what was Jesus' attitude about His success? What did He do after dismissing the crowds? Did He say, as many pastors say, "Now the service is over, I deserve a break?" No, instead He felt the need to go up into a mountain apart to pray.

This is a key to keeping your church on the grow: to pray for the people to whom the pastor has ministered. Charles Finney had an 85% convert retention rate. Most churches today have a 4% retention rate. What was Finney's secret? He did as Jesus did. After dismissing the crowds, he would pray — intercede — for the people to whom he had ministered.

God help us! I know a former minister who is now in prison because when success came to his ministry, he slacked off on his prayer life, yielded to a subtle temptation, and then tried to justify himself in it.

> Watch and PRAY that ye enter not into temptation. (Matthew 26:41)

My associate and I had breakfast with a wise elder minister who has been around since the early days of the "Pentecostal Revivals." He told us that he had known of 200 ministers whom God began using in areas such as miracles and healings. Out of that 200, only three are still in the ministry today! The other 197 drifted off into OBSCURITY. Why? Because pride crept in and prayer fizzled out! The other three are known around the world!

I know of businessmen who have suffered the same consequences.

TIMES OF SUCCESS AND PROSPERITY
CAN BE DANGEROUS IF WE DON'T KEEP
OUR PRIORITIES STRAIGHT

I believe strongly that we are living in an era when God is going to pour "silver and gold" into the churches that are following His direction. A possible time of prosperity is ahead for the Church of Jesus Christ. But it will be a dangerous time, IF we cease to pray and seek God in the midst of the blessings.

This is where the nation Israel always went wrong. Whenever God would prosper her, she would quit calling out to Him and begin to trust in her own devices. It brought destruction every time!

Sometimes prestige, authority, and financial blessings will blind a person to the fact that he's just an ordinary human being. Nobody is a "cut" above anybody else. We are all made of the same stuff! As the group "Daniel Amos" sings, "Jesus died for sinners, losers *and* winners."

Vital to our continued success, prosperity, and blessings of God is the continuation of seeking Him and praying daily. Pray before success. Pray during success. Pray after success comes.

When You Pray | 11

So far, we have glanced into the prayer-life of the most exciting Man in history: Jesus Christ. We received some insight as to why this Man had such a stalwart anointing of power upon His life and ministry. We were enlightened to the fact that Jesus, as the Son of Man gained His power, NOT by virtue of His divinity (though He was divine), but by the quality of His prayer life.

Notice in Acts 10:38 that Jesus didn't do His mighty works by virtue of His deity. The miracles were accomplished by the ANOINTING of the Holy Spirit!

> How God anointed Jesus of Nazareth with the Holy Ghost and with power: who went about doing good, and healing all that were oppressed of the devil; for God was with him. (Acts 10:38)

This is marvelous news for us! Jesus was divine, but He voluntarily set aside His powers of divinity that He might demonstrate to His followers how to function in the flow of the Spirit! He even made this breath-taking statement to His sincere followers:

> In solemn truth I tell you, ANYONE believing in me shall do the same miracles I have done, and even greater ones, because I am going to be with the Father. (John 14:12 TLB)

If Jesus had done His miracles only as a normal function of His deity, He would have never made such a statement as this. The followers of Jesus Christ could have the same powerful anointing that Jesus had in His earthly ministry.

What were some of the astonishing marvels Jesus produced? Let's look:

1. **He changed water into wine** (John 2:1-11). (NOTE: We have received reports from our missionaries in Indonesia that this is frequently happening there! Oftentimes they have no wine for their communion services so they fill containers with water, pray and believe God for a miracle, and the water becomes the finest wine!)

2. **He healed people even from a distance** (John 4:46-54; Matthew 15:21-28).

3. **He miraculously cleansed people suffering with the most dreaded diseases** (Luke 5:12-15; Luke 5:17-20; Luke 8:40-48).

4. **He raised the dead** (Luke 7:11-17; John 11:1-7, 17, 20-27).

5. **He ejected demon spirits from people's lives** (Mark 1:21-27; Mark 5:1-19; Matthew 17:14-18).

6. **He opened blind eyes and unstopped deaf ears** (John 5:1-9; Matthew 9:27-31; Mark 7:32-37; Mark 8:22-26; John 9:1-7).

7. **He cured spinal problems and bone diseases** (Luke 13:11-17).

Think of it! Jesus said, *"ANYONE believing in Me shall do the same miracles I have done, and even greater ones!"* Incredible? Well, there were several apostles — and even some lay people — who believed Jesus AND THE MIRACLES BEGAN (Acts 5:16; Acts 6:8; Acts 8:5-8)!

This power and anointing comes by FAITH! Notice Jesus said, *"Anyone believing...."* If you don't believe miracles can happen today, you'll probably never experience one. But the moment you *believe*, suddenly what is impossible becomes possible.

Faith is built by reading, hearing, studying and meditating upon God's Word. But faith is sharpened as you get to know the Father in prayer. It's sort of like this: Reading the Word will put knowledge into your head. Prayer and meditation will melt the head knowledge and drain it into your heart — your spirit — where it can be turned loose for miracles!

The disciples saw this power in Jesus' life. They watched Him pray. They witnessed His miracles. They knew there was something excitingly different and powerful about His prayer life. They connected the amazing healings and miracles with His seeming *"addiction"* to prayer.

One disciple said, "Teach us to pray." Let's look at Luke 11:1-2:

> [1] And it came to pass that, as he was praying in a certain place, when he ceased, one of his disciples said unto him, Lord, teach us to pray, as John also taught his disciples.
> [2] And he said unto them, When ye pray, say Our Father which art in heaven, Hallowed be thy name. Thy kingdom come. Thy will be done, as in heaven so in earth.

JESUS TEACHES ON THE SUBJECT OF PRAYER

"And He said unto them:

1. *WHEN ye pray....*" Jesus didn't say *if* you pray; He said *when* you pray. A life of prayer is an expected practice for the believer.

2. *"When YE pray...."* Jesus said, *"YOU* pray!" Don't always be depending upon others to pray for you. Learn the secret of prayer yourself!

It's not wrong to ask for prayer from others, but don't be a professional *"pray-for-me."* Some immature believers have never sought knowledge on how to pray for themselves. Instead they try to rely upon others to do their praying. This should not be. It is not acceptable in God's sight. We must each learn to pray for ourselves. Of course, there are times we need to call upon others for added prayer support, but their prayers should only supplement our own prayers, not replace them.

3. *"When ye pray, SAY...."* Jesus did not say, When ye pray, "think." He said, *"SAY."*

"Think-a-prayers" are okay, but Jesus taught us that to be powerful pray-ERs we must not just *"think-a-prayer,"* but *"SAY-a-prayer."* That means to talk when you pray. It's easy for the mind to wander if prayers are not verbalized.

One day, I told my wife I was going into the bedroom to pray. Well, I read my Bible for a while and my eyes became very heavy, so I thought I'd quit reading and pray. It seemed to be too much of an effort to even whisper, so I closed my eyes and tried to *"think"* my prayers. Later my wife woke me up and, jestingly, asked how my prayers were coming! I joked back, *"Oh my! I'm praying so good today, I'm even having visions!"* (Actually they were dreams!) I had fallen asleep trying to *"think"* my prayers.

God understands *"think-a-prayers."* But for our own benefit, it's better to speak them out. And besides that, Jesus said to *"say,"* so that should be reason enough to verbalize our prayers as we are alone in a "secret place" with our Heavenly Father.

Just like a P.A. system in a supermarket, the music may be playing, but when the checkout person needs assistance, the microphone overrides the music. Our words can override the cares, troubles and drifting thoughts that seek to distract us when praying.

So the three important keys found in this chapter are:

1. DO PRAY, GOD EXPECTS YOU TO!
2. LEARN TO PRAY FOR YOURSELF.
3. VERBALIZE YOUR CONVERSATION WITH GOD.

"Our Father" | **12**

Jesus introduced a radical new concept in prayer when He taught His disciples to open in prayer by addressing God as *"Father."*

> After this manner therefore pray ye: Our Father which art in heaven, Hallowed be thy name. (Matthew 6:9)

There are very few scriptural references to God as *"Father of the fatherless."* In Isaiah 9:6, He is cited as the *"Everlasting Father."* There are no more than five other Old Testament references to God as a Father.

But Jesus changed all that when He came along. In the New Testament, Jesus alone referred to GOD AS FATHER more than 70 times!

WHAT DOES THIS TELL US?

This says to us something of great significance. It tells us that prayer for the Christian is *not* to be a religious exercise, but a family conversation. Let me put that in different words:

PRAYER IS NOT TO BE A RELIGIOUS-LIKE APPROACH, BUT A FAMILY-LIKE APPROACH!

We're not part of a religion — we're part of a *FAMILY!* God's family.

¹⁴ For this cause I bow my knees unto the Father of our Lord Jesus Christ,

¹⁵ Of whom the whole family in heaven and earth is named. (Ephesians 3:14-15)

God has family members in heaven and on earth!

Whenever we face a problem with God, it's usually not a problem with theology, but of our understanding and acceptance of the Father's love. Satan's tactic is to corrupt our image of the Father's love.

Dr. Robert Frost has done much ministering on *"The Love of our Heavenly Father."* I encourage you to get his books and tapes on the subject.

One day Dr. Frost was praying with a minister's wife to receive the Holy Spirit Baptism. She was having a difficult time receiving even though she had been praying for this experience for a year. While he prayed for this woman, a thought from the Lord came to him: *"Tell her that I really love her!"*

Dr. Frost followed that thought. He looked at the minister's wife and said, *"I believe the Father would like me to tell you that He really loves you."* Suddenly the lady began weeping and tears started rolling down her face. It was just what she needed to hear because it had been several months since she felt God's love. Satan had convinced her that she wasn't loved by God. She knew what was theologically correct, but in a practical way she didn't believe it. She was totally released through those simple words from Dr. Frost's lips.

All people need to feel loved. It's a basic root-desire in every human being. Every Christian wants to be *"special"* to

God; we want to be loved by Him. So this is a prime target area for Satan to strike. But what causes Satan to distort our concept of God as a loving Heavenly Father?

1.   THEOLOGICAL TRADITION. Sometimes religious leaders can paint a poor picture of the Father's love. The Pharisees, for example, painted a hard, harsh, cold picture of the Father into the minds of the people. They portrayed God as a nit-picking, fault-finding, cold, calculated, finicky old man!

We do the same thing! We visualize the Father as an angry judge and Jesus as our lawyer pleading with Him to overlook our faults. Well the truth of the matter is, God doesn't have to be persuaded to love you. He already loves you. The fact is: the Father was in Christ reconciling the world unto Himself. He suffered for you just as much as Jesus did.

> To wit, that God was in Christ, reconciling the world unto himself, not imputing their trespasses unto them; and hath committed unto us the word of reconciliation. (2 Corinthians 5:19)

Jesus sought to change the false image of His Father that the religious leaders had been propagating. He lived a life of love, doing good, healing people, and showing people the keys to the kingdom. He even said, *"He that hath seen me hath seen the Father!"*

THE FATHER IS *FOR* YOU — NOT AGAINST YOU!

2.   A FAULTY EARTHLY FATHER. Usually we will convey all our earthly father's faults to our mental picture of the Heavenly Father. This shouldn't be.

I remember a young girl whose father was terribly mean. She was afraid of water but her father wanted her to learn to swim so he took her to the middle of the lake in a small boat and threw her overboard, thinking she would learn. The poor girl was terrified. She screamed, she cried, she kicked, she hollered for help. Finally her dad pulled her out of the water.

Parents often don't realize the importance of their role in shaping the character of their child. Recent studies reveal that many of the growing problems that young people face today are a direct result of blurred parental roles.

The truth of the Heavenly Father's love is this:

1. He has no moods. God is never in a "bad mood."
2. His love is unconditional — no strings attached. He loves you no matter what you have done.

Our children disappoint us at times, but we never quit loving them. I remember my two-year-old daughter saying, "Daddy, I wet the bed!" She wasn't afraid to come and tell me because she knew I'd love her anyway. One day she ran up to me and said, "Daddy, I hit David today but I'm really sorry." She had lost her temper with her little brother. But I still love her.

And God still loves you. He's not shocked by your short comings. He's not shocked when you sin! He knows your frame and what you're made of.

Our Father is interested in us and in our welfare.

> If ye then, being evil, know how to give good gifts unto your children, how much more shall your Father which is in heaven give good things to them that ask Him? (Matthew 7:11)

God wants us to enter into prayer with a non-threatening climate. He wants us to take a family-like approach to talking with Him; our Heavenly Father!

What Is God's Address? | 13 |

Several years ago the city newspaper printed a letter from an eight-year-old girl that was addressed to God. The post office had a problem: they didn't know God's address.

What is an address? It's a place where someone resides. If we are to "address" our Father, we must know where He resides.

> After this manner therefore pray ye: Our Father, WHICH ART IN HEAVEN .... (Matthew 6:9)

What is God's address? Where does our Father reside? Jesus told us. He said, *"Which art in Heaven,"* or *"who is in heaven!"* God's address is H-E-A-V-E-N.

But where is heaven ? Where is it located? Does it have a zip code? Let's find out where heaven is located.

WHAT IS HEAVEN'S LOCATION?

1. HERE ON EARTH AND IN THE EARTH'S ATMO-SPHERE. The first realm of heaven invisibly co-exists with the earth and its atmosphere. That's why Jesus said, *"The Kingdom of heaven is at hand"* (Matthew 4:17; 10:7). It's right here at hand.

What is God's address? Right here! Right where you are reading this now. God is in the room with you.

I always wondered what was meant by this Scripture:

> And I will give unto thee the keys of the kingdom of heaven: and whatsoever thou shalt bind on earth shall be bound in heaven: and whatsoever thou shalt loose on earth shall be loosed in heaven. (Matthew 16:19)

Now I know what it means. It means that heaven will back us up all the way when we *"bind"* or *"loose"* something. In other words, if we, being in the natural, visible realm of existence call forth the binding of an evil spirit, the invisible realm of heaven will back us up.

Years ago I experienced a great deal of mental torment from the enemy. I had just launched out into full-time ministry and discovered that my wife was pregnant. Money was tight and the bills were piling up. We prayed, we quoted Scriptures, we made our faith announcement that God would meet all our needs, but I was still going through a real battle.

The devil kept telling me that I'd end up in a gutter with my family. He accused me of being foolish for leaving a good paying job with good benefits. Somehow I knew that God would meet our needs, but the enemy kept telling me how irresponsible I was. I couldn't seem to pray — my mind would drift like an old log on a rough sea.

Finally, I went into the bedroom and said, "I'm going to pray in the Spirit until something happens." I got determined! I began praying in tongues and closed my ears to the enemy. After a few moments a Scripture verse came to me. It was:

> And I will give unto thee the keys of the kingdom of heaven: and whatsoever thou shalt bind on earth shall be bound in heaven: and whatsoever thou shalt loose on earth shall be loosed in heaven.

(Matthew 16:19)

I didn't know what it meant exactly but I screamed, "Father, in Jesus' Name, I hereby loose all the angels necessary to help me bind these voices of darkness." It may sound strange, but INSTANTLY a powerful sense of peace came over me. God met our needs 100%.

Heaven backed me up when I *"loosed"* some invisible reinforcements!

A friend of mine who is a leader in an Assemblies of God church in Michigan related an interesting incident to me. A spiritualist woman visited the church and lured some people into a "side show" on the church property.

She was demonstrating her "psychic power" to control material objects. Someone would hold a watch or a chain up to her face. She would "concentrate" and the watch would begin to swing, almost violently. Well, a fine Christian man knew this power was not from God, but from an evil source, and not wanting any of the new Christians to be deceived, he simply said, "In the Name of Jesus Christ, I bind you, devil!" Just then the watch quit swinging. The *"power"* had been broken. Heaven backed him up!

What is God's address? It's heaven! And the first realm of heaven co-exists with this natural material world. That means that GOD IS NEAR. When you pray, be assured, God is near!

God's Address, Part II | **14**

God's address is heaven! The first realm of heaven co-exists with this natural world. But there are other realms of heaven. The second realm is much broader than the first.

> [1] The heavens declare the glory of God; and the firmament sheweth his handiwork.
> [2] Day unto day uttereth speech, and night unto night sheweth knowledge.
> [6] His going forth is from the end of heaven, and his circuit unto the ends of it: and there is nothing hid from the heat thereof. (Psalm 19:1,2,6)

The second realm of heaven includes the entire universe; the stars, the planets, the galaxies, and the extremities of outer space.

God is patrolling the universe, we are told in verse six. He has a regular circuit. And He travels faster than Bell Telephone or Western Union.

Go out at night and look into the sky ... the heavens. Stop and think: God created it all. He is BIG! If you could travel at 186,000 miles per second and travel at that speed, for a whole year, you would only be on the edge of our galaxy! And think of it; there are a billion or more galaxies bigger than ours. And God can patrol the whole thing in less than a micro second!

When we see the bigness of our Father and His creation, we can understand how He is able to help us. (Read Psalm 12:1-8.)

When the Early Christians had a problem, the first thing they did was focus upon the bigness of their heavenly Father. They didn't even make their request until they had a good foundation of the BIGNESS of God. Look at their prayer in Acts 4:24:

> And when they heard that, they lifted up their voice to God with one accord, and said, Lord, thou art God which hast made heaven, and earth, and the sea, and all that in them is. (Acts 4:24)

They focused upon the bigness of the Father. Only looking at our shortcomings, weaknesses, or difficult situations can paralyze us. But looking at our Father's greatness can lift us!

A man was on the roof of the house doing some work when he heard his eleven-year-old son screaming. The dad looked over the side of the roof and there was his son halfway up the ladder, frantically hanging on for dear life. The father said, "Come on up, son." The boy replied, "I can't!"

"Yes, you can, son. Just quit looking down. Keep your eyes on me."

Sure enough the youngster made it by keeping his eyes on his father. That's how we can make it too! By not looking down — but looking UP.

When I'm facing pressing issues and when problems seem to be surrounding me on all sides, I sometimes use a little faith exercise. I kneel down (or sit down), close my eyes and pretend I'm slowly rising away from earth. I see it getting smaller and smaller. I think, *God, You created that globe. And You created me. Certainly nothing is too hard for You.* It gives me a better perspective on things when I do that.

And don't forget! The same God who created the whole universe lives in you!

> Now unto him that is able to do exceeding abundantly above all that we ask or think, according to the power that worketh in us. (Ephesians 3:20)

John G. Lake, that famous missionary who was mightily used of God in the 1930's and 40's used to get up every morning, get dressed, look into a mirror and say, "Everywhere this suit goes, God goes."

He understood the truth of having the God who created the universe living right inside of him.

> Know ye not that ye are the temple of God, and that the Spirit of God dwelleth in you? (I Corinthians 3:16)

What is God's address?

1st realm — Right here, which tells us, "God is near!"
2nd realm — The universe, which tells us, "God is able."

In the next chapter we'll look at the 3rd realm of heaven.

God's Address, Part III 15

I knew a man in Christ above, fourteen years ago, (whether in the body, I cannot tell; or whether out of the body, I cannot tell: God knoweth;) such an one caught up to the third heaven. (2 Corinthians 12:2)

[1] Let not your heart be troubled: ye believe in God, believe also in me.

[2] In my Father's house are many mansions: if it were not so, I would have told you. I go to prepare a place for you.

[3] And if I go and prepare a place for you, I will come again, and receive you unto myself; that where I am, there ye may be also. (John 14:1-3)

The third realm of heaven is a PLACE. It's an actual place! Here's the way the Bible describes the third heaven:

1. It's a *place*, not just a misty, cloudy, eerie-type of fog somewhere. Heaven is an actual place (John 14:1-3).

2. It's a *country*, which indicates its vastness. There's enough room for everybody who accepts Christ! (Hebrews 11:9,14,15,16)

3. It's a *city*, implying a large number of people. This also tells us that business goes on in heaven (Revelation 3:12, 22:14,19; Hebrews 11:16).

4. It's a *kingdom*, which tells us that there is order in heaven. (Matthew 13)

5. It's a *paradise*, with no deception; no devil. (Luke 23:43)

6. It's the *Father's house*, indicating its eternal nature.

Here's a good exercise: when you pray, think of yourself in the family room at the Father's house. Often we think of God on a huge throne with smoke and fog all around Him. Well He *is* on a throne, but the throne is in His house! Relax before the Father. You are part of His family.

The third heaven is our destination. We sing that song, "This world is not my home, I'm just passing through!" I like that. The Bible calls us believers *"pilgrims."* We're on a journey to another land.

I conducted a funeral service for a precious Christian lady this year. Someone said to her 82-year-old husband, "I'm sorry you lost your wife." He responded, "Oh, I didn't lose her. I know right where she's at." She just received a transfer to the third heaven.

When we visualize God's address at the third realm of heaven, we'll find ourselves making decisions in light of our eternal home. Life here on earth is like a drop of water compared to the ocean of eternal life found in Jesus Christ.

What is God's address?

1. Among you.
2. In the entire universe.
3. At the home called heaven!

God's Name and Holiness 16

Hallowed be thy name. (Matthew 6:9)

The focus of this phrase is upon two things:

1. God's Name.
2. God's Holiness.

Why do you suppose Jesus wanted us to focus on God's name? Could it be because a name implies a personality? Of course. It was because Jesus wanted us to concentrate on our Heavenly Father as a Person, not some sort of abstract "being."

I am amazed at the names unregenerated people give to God. Notice how nebulous and non-personal these names are:

- "The Universal Mind"
- "The Infinite Intelligence"
- "The Mystical Influence"
- "The Divine Principle"
- "The Supreme Being"

Usually it is cult leaders who give such cold names to God. God is not a Universal Mind or a Divine Principle — HE IS A PERSON, A DIVINE PERSON! HE has a name!

There's something so very personal about a name. Nobody wants his or her name misspelled in a newspaper (or anywhere else, for that matter).

When I was in the U.S. Navy, one of my functions aboard the *U.S.S. Reasoner* was to take charge of the ship's newspaper. I was the editor-in-chief.

I ran some interesting experiments while I was editor of that paper. One experiment included deliberately misspelling a person's name week after week. His name was Brandl (pronounced Bran-Dull). We made sure we had a story about Brandl every week. The first week we spelled his name "B-R-A-N-D-E-L-L." That wasn't too bad. The next week: "B-R-A-N-D-A-L-L." The next: "B-R-A-N-D-X." It was hilarious to all the sailors except one: Brandl.

People would see Brandl coming down the ship's passageway and holler, "Hey! How's it going, Brand-X!"

Finally, Brandl could take it no longer. He stormed out of his division compartment in search of the ship's news editor. He found me, grabbed me by the shirt and shook me while he screeched with disgust something to this effect: "Ever since I've been in the Navy I've had nothing! No home, no car, no money. The only thing I have is my name and you are trying to take that away from me!"

Needless to say, I learned fast that people's names are important to them.

A name is very personal. God has a name. If God were just a principle, you couldn't reason with Him. But since He is a

Person, you can actually reason with God.

> Come now, and let us reason together, saith the Lord: though your sins be as scarlet, they shall be as white as snow; though they be red like crimson, they shall be as wool. (Isaiah 1:18)

HIS NAME MEANS SOMETHING

Names don't always mean much today. A boy named "George Washington" might be the biggest liar you ever met. A used car dealer named "Honest Abe" might not be so honest. Many people who were named after saints became drunkards or derelicts.

But with a careful study of God's name, we can get no false impressions of His character. You see, when the Bible was written, names were given to people to describe their character or nature. In fact God changed some people's names in order to better describe their character. Names had significance.

God's name has more significance than any other name. In fact, God has to have several names to describe Himself to human beings. Here are a few of those names and their meanings.

- Elohim — Creator
- El Shaddai — mighty, powerful, nourisher & supplier (The God who is more than enough.)
- Jehovah Jireh — the promise keeper.
- Jehovah Shalom — the God of peace.
- I AM — The Eternal One, the God of the "NOW."

Now Jesus said something very interesting to the Pharisees:

Before Abraham was, I AM. (John 8:58)

When Jesus said that, Abraham had been dead for several hundred years. Could this mean that Jesus is also God? It's strange, but He voiced no opposition to Thomas' bold statement, "My Lord and My God!" (John 20:28)

When we think of the Name of God, we think of the Name of Jesus! Look at this:

- **ELOHIM** (Creator) — Colossians 1:16 "For by him [Jesus Christ] were all things created, that are in heaven, and that are in earth, visible and invisible, whether they be thrones or dominions, or principalities, or powers: all things were created by him and for him."

- **EL SHADDAI** (Supplier) — Philippians 4:19: "But my God shall supply all your need according to his riches in glory BY CHRIST JESUS."

- **JEHOVAH JIREH** (Promise Keeper) — 2 Corinthians 1:20: "For all the promises of God in him (CHRIST JESUS) are yea, and in him (CHRIST JESUS) Amen, unto the glory of God by us."

- **JEHOVAH SHALOM** (Peace Giver) — John 14:27 (Words of Jesus): "Peace I leave with you, my peace I give unto you: not as the world giveth, give I unto you. Let not your heart be troubled, neither let it be afraid."

- **I AM** (Eternal One) — Philippians 2:9-11: "Wherefore God also hath highly exalted him, and given him a name which is above every name: That at the name of Jesus every knee should bow, of things in heaven and things in earth, and things under the earth; and that every tongue should confess that Jesus Christ is Lord, to the glory of God the Father."

Concentrating on the Name of Jesus as the Name of God, we begin to see all the availabilities to us as believers.

I know of a lady who claimed the promise of Mark 16:18 when her young son accidentally drank some poison. She said, "Father, in Jesus' Name, You said, `If they drink any deadly thing it will not hurt them.'" The little boy had no reaction after she claimed her rights in Jesus' Name.

A woman missionary was stung by a deadly scorpion. There was no known antidote. The sting was almost always fatal. But she claimed the promise of Mark 16:18 and in the Name of Jesus shook the creature off, and never had any adverse reaction.

In Acts chapter three, Peter told a lame man, "In the NAME of Jesus Christ of Nazareth, rise up and walk!" And the man walked.

With all of the good found in God's Name, and all the benefits of understanding His Name and being permitted to use His Name, why do some people neither respect it nor honor it? Why do they downgrade God? Why do they curse God? Why do they take His Name in vain?

The reason is because when people hear God's Name, they know it stands for holiness and purity. They begin to see themselves in light of a holy God which leads them to one of two reactions:

1. Rebellion (or)
2. Repentance

After Isaiah, a prophet of God, caught a glimpse of God's holiness, he said, "I'm a man of unclean lips." Read Isaiah 6:1-5 and see what happens to a person who sees God's glory and holiness.

Every revival ever recorded in history has involved a glimpse into the Name and holiness of God. Understanding these two aspects of God will prompt us to receive power through faith-filled prayer! Study God's Name, learn of His holiness. Then pray, "Lord, make me more like You!"

REVIVAL

I know an evangelist who was conducting a series of special services in a small, rather dead-type church. He prayed and sought the Lord for revival but nothing — I mean nothing — appeared to be happening in that church. Nobody was getting saved. Nobody was getting healed. Nobody was getting filled with the Holy Spirit. The evangelist felt terrible! He didn't know what was wrong.

Eleven days and nights passed. On the twelfth evening, the preacher decided it was no use. He would preach one more message, then pack up and go. But that night something happened. God began to reveal His holiness to the people. It wasn't something you could see, but the Presence was real.

An eleven-year-old stood up with tears in her eyes and said, "Excuse me, I'm sorry to interrupt you Brother, but I've gotta apologize to my Sunday School teacher, `I'm so sorry

Mrs. Smith, for being so bad in your class. Will you forgive me?'"

This started a chain reaction! The people began to apologize to each other for even the smallest things. They called to God and asked His forgiveness. Revival came like a flash flood. People were crying and rejoicing in the Name and holiness of God.

That night six people walked into that building and accepted Christ! They had no idea why they even came! But Jesus changed their lives.

You see, that little church finally caught a fresh glimpse of God's holiness. They responded by genuine repentance and God saw that they were in a position to receive revival and be greatly used by Him!

What is the secret of power with God? It is partly found in understanding and functioning in the Name and holiness of our God.

The Coming World of Tomorrow | 17

Thy kingdom come .... (Matthew 6:10)

Each week millions of people pray, "Thy kingdom come," without any serious intention of it happening. Others pray it without even knowing what it means.

What is meant by "God's Kingdom?" Scholarly theologians and commentators debate about what Jesus meant when He told us to pray "Thy kingdom come." All have some good points, worthy of recognition.

WORLD EVANGELISM

One Bible scholar believes that this statement is a request for world evangelization; that God's Kingdom would come to hearts and lives around the globe. The request is for HIS Kingdom to come; not our own.

In other words, Jesus did not say to pray for "the kingdom of the Assemblies of God" to come. Nor did He say to pray for "the kingdom of the general Baptists" to come, nor "the kingdom of Catholicism" or "Lutheranism" or "Methodism." He said to pray for God's Kingdom to come. Should He choose to use Baptists, Methodists, or Lutherans in bringing about His kingdom (world evangelization), then let Him do it! God is God and can use any believer who is open to His Spirit and willing to be obedient.

KINGDOM AGE

Other theologians believe that Jesus is referring to the coming Kingdom Age, when Jesus will return to earth to rule and reign from Jerusalem.

OTHER VIEWS

Still other commentators admit they don't know if Jesus was referring to the Kingdom of God or the Kingdom of Heaven. There are different schools of theology on this subject. Some believe there are two distinctly different Kingdoms.

Theologian "A" says:

1. The Kingdom of God is the invisible Kingdom now on the earth whereas,

2. The Kingdom of Heaven refers to the future Kingdom.

Theologian "B" says:

1. The Kingdom of God is the entire sphere of professing Christianity, whereas,

2. The Kingdom of Heaven refers only to those genuine Christians who are born again.

These are all interesting viewpoints, worthy of further study, however the real issue is not which Kingdom Jesus was talking about but WHOSE Kingdom He was talking about! He said to pray to the Father, "Thy Kingdom come," or in modern language, "Your Kingdom come!"

The important issue here is that we are praying that God's Kingdom will come. If it's God's Kingdom, that means it's not man's kingdom. Man's kingdom has a beginning and an ending so there's no sense in putting our trust or hope in man's kingdom.

I was just reading the economist's predictions for our national budget. It said that the United States deficit will probably run over four trillion dollars. That means that if every person IN THE ENTIRE WORLD gave $600.00 each to the U.S., we still wouldn't be out of debt! Economic confusion is hanging over our country like a dark fog. It illustrates to us how futile it is to place our faith in man's kingdom.

Historians tell us there have been 21 great earthly kingdoms in all of recorded history. They rose. They fell. But all the while these kingdoms were rising and falling, God's Kingdom went on and still goes on — it's eternal.

   [8] The Lord is gracious, and full of compassion; slow to anger, and of great mercy.
   [9] The Lord is good to all: and his tender mercies are over all his works.
   [10] All thy works shall praise thee, O Lord; and thy saints shall bless thee.
   [11] They shall speak of the glory of thy kingdom, and talk of thy power;
   [12] To make known to the sons of men his mighty acts, and the glorious majesty of his kingdom.
   [13] Thy kingdom is an everlasting kingdom, and thy dominion endureth throughout all generations. (Psalm 145: 8-13)

One thing we know for sure; It's good to be a part of a Kingdom that can't fall. God's Kingdom is eternal. It's not subject to depression and recession and inflation. That's why God (the King) never has any problem providing for His people (the subjects of His Kingdom), when hard times come. Because God's supply system does not depend upon our economy.

TWO ASPECTS OF THE KINGDOM

There are two aspects of God's Kingdom we should look into:

1. Future Phase.
2. Present Phase.

Let's start with the future phase of God's Kingdom.

There is coming a day when Jesus will return to earth and rule for 1000 years! This is known as the Kingdom Age. We look forward to this age with great anticipation.

Let's look at some interesting facts about the coming "Kingdom Age."

1. The devil will be bound for 1000 years! (Revelation 20:1-3)
2. There will be no war. (Isaiah 2:1-4; Micah 4:3-4)
3. Animals will be friendly. Even poisonous snakes will not bite people. (Isaiah 11:6)
4. Jesus will rule the nations. (Revelation 19:15; Psalm 72:12-14)

MISCONCEPTIONS

There are many misconceptions concerning the coming Kingdom Age. One of the most devilish is that the Kingdom Age began in 1914. How can any intelligent human being make such a foolish observation? How can anyone say the devil is bound?

I visited the hospital to pray with a young man who sliced his arms with a razor blade and then stuck coat hangers up his veins. The devil is still on the loose! I visited a lady who was writhing in pain from a cancerous tumor. The warfare is still on!

> For we wrestle not against flesh and blood, but against principalities, against powers, against the rulers of the darkness of this world, against spiritual wickedness in high places. (Ephesians 6:12)

The devil is still on the rampage, out to devour anyone who will take what he offers! (1 Peter 5:8)

A second misconception is that the Kingdom Age will gradually be ushered in as we offer educational, social, and economic development to all nations. Or when all Christians are in government, "discipling the nations." It is a popular teaching today that Christians will gradually take over the governments of the world to set the stage for Jesus to come back.

But Jesus taught something quite different. He taught that the Kingdom Age would be born with birth pangs. He said there would be wars, famines, pestilences, earthquakes, disease, etc. (Matthew 24, Mark 13, Luke 21)

In fact at the beginning of the Kingdom Age there will probably be less than a billion people left alive on earth because of the wars and judgements. (Revelation 6:8; Revelation 9:18)

WHEN?

When will this Kingdom Age come? Here's a list of chronological events I believe to be accurate.

Bible Prophecy Charts

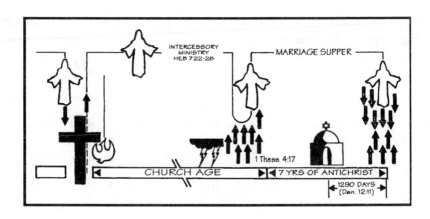

INTERCESSORY MINISTRY HEB.7:22-28

MARRIAGE SUPPER

1 Thess. 4:17

CHURCH AGE

7 YRS OF ANTICHRIST

1290 DAYS (Dan. 12:11)

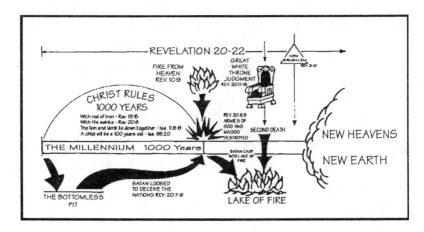

REVELATION 20-22

NEW JERUSALEM REV. 21:10

FIRE FROM HEAVEN REV. 10:9

GREAT WHITE THRONE JUDGMENT REV. 20:11-15

CHRIST RULES 1000 YEARS

With rod of iron - Rev. 19:15
With His saints - Rev. 20:6
The lion and lamb lie down together - Isa. 11.6-9
A child will be a 100 years old - Isa. 65:20

REV. 20.8,9 ARMIES OF GOG AND MAGOG DESTROYED

SECOND DEATH

NEW HEAVENS

THE MILLENNIUM 1000 Years

SATAN CAST INTO LAKE OF FIRE

NEW EARTH

THE BOTTOMLESS PIT

SATAN LOOSED TO DECEIVE THE NATIONS REV. 20:7-9

LAKE OF FIRE

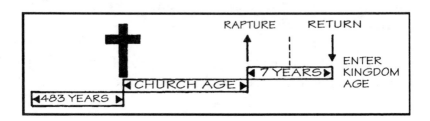

RAPTURE

RETURN

7 YEARS

ENTER KINGDOM AGE

CHURCH AGE

483 YEARS

1. The Rapture (Catching Away) of believers who love Jesus and are walking in all the light they have. Jesus will not return to earth at this time - only as far as the clouds to call us upward! (1 Thessalonians 4:13-18; 1 Corinthians 15:51-52)

2. Northern nations invade Israel, leading to possible World War III. (Ezekiel 38 & 39)

3. 10-Nation European Common Market rises to world economic power! (Daniel 2)

4. World leader arises with all the right answers — world government and world monetary system will be the order (1 John 2:18; 2 Thessalonians 2: 3-12). Some will call this the "New World Order."

5. Short span of peace and security on earth. (1 Thessalonians 5:3)

6. Greatest bloodbath in the history of the world (Matthew 24:21). Persecution of Jews and Christians.

7. Finally, all the armies assemble for the last war. (Armageddon — Revelation 16:16)

8. Jesus sends angels to gather up the elect — those who accepted Christ during the persecution. (Matthew 24:31)

9. Jesus returns with His people to earth!

10. Nations are judged and we enter into the Kingdom Age. (Isaiah 2:1-4)

But who will be on earth for the Kingdom Age?

1. Those who survived the Great Tribulation. They will be servants and general laborers during the 1000-year Kingdom Age.

2. Christians with glorified bodies!

Beloved, now are we the sons of God, and it doth not yet appear what we shall be: but we know that, when he shall appear, we shall be like him; for we shall see him as he is. (1 John 3:2)

We shall have bodies similar to that of Jesus. (1 Corinthians 15:35-49; 1 John 3:2)

1. We will be able to defy natural laws such as gravity. (Acts 1:9; 1 Thessalonians 4:17)

2. We will be able to be transported instantly to another location if we desire or are needed. (Acts 8:35-40; Luke 24:31)

3. We will have recognition of each other. (John 20:19-29)

4. We will appear the same as we do now; to have physical-looking bodies. (John 20-27)

5. We will be able to walk through closed doors and walls. (John 20:19)

6. We will be able to eat and drink. (John 21:1-14)

7. There will be no death for those who have received glorified bodies! (Luke 20:36)

There will be death for those tribulation survivors and their children during the Kingdom Age. Death resides in every physical body just waiting to take over. It will be the last enemy to be destroyed. (1 Corinthians 15:26; Revelation 20:14)

Notice in Isaiah 65:20, we're told that there will still be some "sinners" in the world even during the Kingdom Age.

There shall be no more thence an infant of days, nor an old man that hath not filled his days: for the child shall die an hundred years old; but the sinner being an hundred years old shall be accursed.

It will not be a perfect age, however, it will be an age to prove that peace could have prevailed all these thousands of years if only we would have sought God's Kingship instead of our own.

GOVERNMENT

What about the Kingdom government? It will be 100% Christian! The generals, majors, councilmen, governors, senators will all be appointed by Jesus Himself! (Isaiah 2:2,4)

Jesus will be the president of the world. (Psalm 48:1-3) Every year delegates will go to Jerusalem to make annual reports. We will attend the Feast of Tabernacles (Zechariah 14:16) where Jesus, Himself will be the keynote speaker! What a conference!

What will determine our position during the Kingdom Age? Luke 19:17 indicates that our faithfulness to God's will here and now determines our Kingdom position.

But you can't be a part of this future phase of the Kingdom if you don't join this present phase of the Kingdom, Jesus said:

> Jesus answered and said unto him, Verily, verily, I say unto thee, Except a man be born again he cannot see the Kingdom of God. (John 3:3)

If you are not sure that you're a born-again believer, ask the Father to make you part of His Kingdom by receiving Christ as Lord.

If you are a born-again believer, pray that the Kingdom will come to people's hearts and lives around the world. Pray for world missions. Pray for GOD'S KINGDOM TO COME!

God's Will Or Some Other Will? | 18

Have you ever wondered what God's plan and purpose is and how it includes and involves you? In the following chapters, I will share with you three basic steps to knowing God's will. These steps are simple and fail-proof; they work 100% of the time.

In continuing our study on the Lord's model prayer, we discover that the request for the Father's will to be done is at the very heart of the prayer.

> Thy will be done in earth, as it is in heaven. (Matthew 6:10)

In prayer, if we are to acquire power with God, it is needful that we consider HIS WILL above all else. This is not an uninteresting or unpleasant task, but an adventurous, stimulating, rewarding venture!

GOD'S WILL IS PERFECT

> As for God, his way is perfect. (2 Samuel 22:31)

God's way is PERFECT. The reason for so much turmoil and uncertainty in the world today is because people have chosen to follow man's will instead of God's will. Man's will is not perfect; God's will is.

Things used to operate in the sphere of God's will. Several thousand, perhaps even a million years ago, the entire universe was moving with perfection in the orbit of God's will. But one day, Lucifer, a created angelic being, decided that he would introduce his will into the universe. As a created being with the God-given privilege to choose, he used this capacity to follow his own will instead of God's.

> [12] How art thou fallen from heaven O Lucifer, son of the morning! How art thou cut down to the ground, which didst weaken the nations!
> [14] For thou hast said in thine heart, I will ascend into heaven, I will exalt my throne above the stars of God: I will sit also upon the mount of the congregation, in the sides of the north:
> [15] I will ascend above the heights of the clouds; I will be like the most High. (Isaiah 14: 12-14)

Notice that Lucifer's underlying sin was that of self-will. Five times he said, "I will." He said, "*I will* take over the government of heaven because I can run things better myself. I'll just push God out of the way and become God myself." But look what God said in reply to this rebellious act of self-will:

> Thou shalt be brought down to hell, to the sides of the pit. (Isaiah 14:15)

So Lucifer was cast out of heaven and became the dreaded creature known as Satan. Now there are two wills in the universe: one perfect; one corrupt. And ever since that day there have been essentially two wills: one perfect; one corrupt.

COMPARTMENTS?

We make a serious mistake when we begin to compartmentalize "wills." For example, we picture several different compartments with doors. We visualize signs on the doors of these compartments:

1. The will of Satan.
2. The will of man.
3. The self will.
4. The good will of God.
5. The acceptable will of God.
6. The permissive will of God.
7. The perfect will of God.

We see this vast array of compartments and figure that we can choose any door as long as it's not the will of Satan—*that's the road to ruin,* we think. *Of course, the permissive will of God is fine,* we reason, *that's only one notch away from God's perfect will!*

Well, as far as I can tell from Scripture, anyone who ever settled for God's so-called *"permissive will,"* actually settled for second best and ended up destroying their lives. For example:

1. Adam and Eve were *permitted* to partake of the forbidden fruit. But they lost their paradise home and their eldest son became a rebel and a murderer.

2. Some of the children of Israel chose *"God's permissive will,"* and ended up dying in the wilderness. (Only those who followed God's *perfect* will went into the Promised Land.)

3. Saul followed the *"permissive will of God"* and ended up committing suicide.

The truth of the matter is this: Anything that is not the PERFECT WILL of God is a CORRUPTED WILL, and can only bring tragedy, heartbreak, and a grim existence. There are basically two doors still today: the door of God's will, and the door of some other will. Selecting the door to God's perfect will is the doorway to success, adventure, excitement and reward. The other door (call it what you like) is the door to disaster.

In the following chapters, we shall learn three basic keys to discerning God's perfect will.

Remember, there are only two wills from which to choose: God's will or some other will. One is perfect; one is corrupt.

Three Steps to Discerning God's Will, Part I **19**

The first step to discerning God's will in any given situation is this:

RECOGNIZE THAT ALL MATTERS OF MORAL AND SPIRITUAL PRINCIPLE ARE CLEARLY DEALT WITH IN THE SCRIPTURES.

> The entrance of thy words giveth light; it giveth understanding unto the simple. (Psalm 119:130)

We don't even have to pray about matters that are clearly dealt with in the Bible. For example, I don't have to beg God to show me His will concerning tithing. He has already spoken His will in His Word. (Malachi 3:8-11)

For the turned-on believer (the "one-hundred percenter") life is very simple. Either something IS the will of God or it ISN'T. There's no in-between. People who stay close to Jesus don't have to search for ways of justifying a wrong. They simply call a sin a sin.

My wife telephoned our local community college because we heard they were sponsoring an obscene play. She talked with the president's secretary and told her that it wasn't right for a responsible, reputable college to sponsor obscenity under the guise of art.

The secretary was a pleasant lady, but immediately started trying to play down the seriousness of their nude production. She said, "Well, only a few of the cast members will disrobe and it's all done in subdued lighting and in very good taste."

Isn't it amazing how people will try to justify their sins and downplay their wrong doings? But to the sincere Christian, wrong is wrong and right is right — it's that simple.

GOD'S WILL CONCERNING SIN

What is God's will concerning sin? The answer is found right there in His Word. But many people have refused to obey God's will as revealed through the Scriptures, consequently, they have not been led any further.

Don't pray about whether or not it's God's will for you to steal, lie or cheat. It's all there in the Bible — clear and simple.

[9,10] Don't you know that those doing such things have no share in the Kingdom of God? Don't fool yourselves. Those who live immoral lives, who are idol worshipers, adulterers or homosexuals — will have no share in his kingdom. Neither will thieves or greedy people, drunkards, slanderers, or robbers. (1 Corinthians 6:9-10 TLB)

[19] But when you follow your own wrong inclinations your lives will produce these evil results: impure thoughts, eagerness for lustful pleasure, [20] idolatry, spiritism (that is, encouraging the activity of demons), hatred and fighting, jealousy and anger, constant effort to get the best for yourself, complaints and criticisms, the feeling that everyone else is wrong except those in your own little group — and there will be wrong doctrine [21] envy, murder, drunkenness, wild parties, and all that sort of thing, let me tell you again as I have before, that anyone living that sort of life will not inherit the Kingdom of God. (Galatians 5:19-21 TLB)

I've been in many rooms with dying people. And the one thing that really matters at death is whether or not they've done God's will. All else is of little importance because now eternity stares them in the face, waiting to snatch their souls from this earth.

> Not every one that saith unto me, Lord, Lord shall enter into the kingdom of heaven; but he that DOETH the will of my Father which is in heaven. (Matthew 7:21)

Jesus Christ and His shed blood is the only thing that can cleanse you of all past sins and give you a clean slate. God's will is for you to follow Jesus Christ.

MARRIAGE

What is God's will concerning marriage? He tells Christians:

> Be not unequally yoked together with unbelievers: for what fellowship hath righteousness with unrighteousness? and what communion hath light with darkness? (2 Corinthians 6:14)

A young Pentecostal girl went against her father's desires when she began dating a non-Christian boy. Her father, being a pastor, had preached on several occasions about the heart-break of being "unequally yoked together with unbelievers." He never suggested that Christians should separate from their unbelieving mates, only that single people place a top-priority on finding a Christian mate.

But this young lady chose to pursue her own way instead of God's perfect way. One night she and her boyfriend were at the parsonage and her dad was talking with the young man. Suddenly, for unknown reasons, the boy went into a rage, pulled a knife and stabbed the girl's father. The boy ran. Moments later, officials tried to save the pastor's life but, alas, it was too late. He was dead!

Yes, it's true. Your sins do affect others! In the Bible, a man named Achan committed a sin — seemingly so private and harmless. But his sin resulted in 36 lives being needlessly lost in battle. A few days later his whole family perished! (Joshua, Chapters 7 and 8)

Sin is insane! Christians who aren't growing and moving ahead have either missed or ignored God's will. Or they have not walked in all the light God has given them concerning the Scriptures. To even consider a marriage outside of God's will is to SIN, and a costly one at that.

GOD'S WILL FOR HEALING

Without going into all the Scriptures that promise healing, let us in this quick study look at Jesus' life! Did He ever refuse healing to anyone who asked in faith? Did He not say Himself, "My meat is to do the will of him that sent me?" (John 4:34)

Jesus did come to do the will of the Father, and He spent a good portion of His ministry healing the sick.

> How God anointed Jesus of Nazareth with the Holy Ghost and with power: who went about doing good, and healing all that were oppressed of the devil; for God was with him. (Acts 10:38)

Martin Luther understood that healing and health are part of God's will. He didn't have to pray the escape-prayer, "Lord, heal, if it be Thy will." (I call this the "escape - prayer" because people use it to escape embarrassment instead of turning their faith loose for another's healing. If the person they pray for doesn't get well, they say, "It wasn't God's will.") The Bible says, "The prayer of FAITH shall save the sick." You can't pray a prayer of FAITH without knowing what God's perfect will is concerning a matter.

Martin Luther didn't dilly-dally around with "escape prayers." He even went further than prayer; he made FAITH COMMANDS. In 1540, Luther's assistant, Frederick Myconius, became ill and was expected to die. On his bed he wrote Luther a farewell letter with his trembling hand. Luther instantly sent back a reply:

> I command you in the Name of God to live because I still have need of you... The Lord will never let me hear that you are dead, but will permit you to survive me.... This is my will, and my will be done, because I seek only to glorify the Name of God. (Notice, Martin Luther expressed his will, which was in perfect harmony with the Lord's will.)

When Myconius read Luther's letter, he began to recover. He was healed and went on to outlive Luther! This is the power of knowing God's will and, yes, even commanding God's will to be done, just as Jesus commanded the storms to calm and the fig tree to shrivel.

The will of God is so exciting! It's where the power is. It's where the action is!

Step number one to discerning God's will is to RECOGNIZE THAT ALL MATTERS OF MORAL AND SPIRITUAL PRINCIPLE ARE CLEARLY DEALT WITH IN THE SCRIPTURES.

Three Steps to Discerning God's Will, Part II 20

The first step to discerning God's will is to understand that all moral and spiritual principles are clearly dealt with in the Scriptures. We learn from the Bible God's general will.

The second step is to PRAY AND TRUST THE HOLY SPIRIT TO WORK WITH YOU.

The person who daily calls upon the Lord in prayer, will begin to see God's plan unfold like a blueprint. He'll find himself becoming increasingly accurate in his daily decisions.

Several years ago, I found myself praying for a new Olds Omega. I would picture myself driving it down the road. As weeks went by, I would pray that God would send that Omega, but discovered that I didn't really want it anymore. For some reason my desire was changed from an Omega to a Chevette, so I began praying for a Chevette. A few weeks later, I got a Chevette! (Omega's are excellent automobiles, but it wasn't God's will for me to have one at the time, so God, through prayer, changed my desire!)

> "Delight thyself also in the Lord; and he shall give thee the desires of thine heart" (Psalm 37:4).

> For it is God which worketh in you both to will and to do of his good pleasure. (Philippians 2:13)

Let God work with you in prayer. Don't go into prayer with your mind already made up as to what He is going to say. *Let* God work; don't try to *MAKE* Him work.

Finally, the third step to knowing God's will is to WAIT FOR CONFIRMATION! God will generally confirm His will in several different ways. Before I launched into the full-time ministry, God confirmed the move no less than 17 times. It seemed that every Scripture pointed to full-time ministry. Every book I would read seemed to tell me to "GO LAUNCH OUT INTO THE DEEP!" Reasonable, spiritual people also confirmed the move of God upon my life.

God will give you several confirmations concerning His will. He's not in a hurry as long as you are not just plain stubborn and rebellious. But you must pray diligently that God will reveal His plan and purpose to your heart. And He'll do it!

While I was praying about the church, God began to give me a supernatural "KNOWING" and assurance concerning His next great movement in the body of Christ. I shared this with my associate and learned that he had been receiving the same supernatural knowledge in prayer. So it was confirmed. But then, an internationally known minister came to our church and told us that God was speaking the exact same thing to his heart. Confirmed again! Now we have discovered that Christian leaders around the world have been receiving the same "revelation from heaven" concerning God's next emphasis in the Church. This guidance and direction comes only through a day-to-day contact with the Father.

In summary, there are essentially two wills from which to choose. First, there is God's will, which is perfect and leads to happiness, contentment, adventure and POWER WITH GOD! Or there is some other will — a corrupt will — which leads only to frustration gloom, and a grim existence.

The three keys to discerning the Lord's perfect will are:

1. SCRIPTURES
2. PRAYER
3. CONFIRMATION

God's Interests | **21**

After this manner therefore pray ye: Our Father which art in heaven, Hallowed be thy name. Thy Kingdom come. Thy will be done in earth, as it is in heaven. Give us this day our daily bread. And forgive us our debts, as we forgive our debtors. And lead us not into temptation, but deliver us from evil: For thine is the kingdom, and the power, and the glory, for ever. Amen. (Matthew 6: 9-13)

Some argue whether or not this prayer is to be used under the new covenant. But, I think the important thing about this model prayer is that we learn to extract principles — divine truths — from it and apply these truths to our personal lives of prayer.

One of the great lessons of prayer and THE SECRET OF POWER WITH GOD taught in this model prayer is to PUT GOD'S INTERESTS FIRST!

There are six requests made in this prayer. The first three involve *God's* interests. The latter three involve *our* personal interests. Also notice the different types of prayer used in Jesus' model prayer.

FIRST THREE REQUESTS (God's interests):

1. "Hallowed be **THY** name" (Prayer of worship).

2. "**THY** Kingdom come." (Prayer of intercession)
3. "**THY** will be done." (Prayer of supplication and commitment)

SECOND THREE REQUESTS (Our interests):

1. "Give **US** our daily bread." (Prayer of petition)
2. "Forgive **US** our debts." (Prayer of confession)
3. "Lead **US** not into temptation but deliver US from evil." (Prayer of warfare and deliverance)

As one grows in prayer, he will soon discover that his own personal interests and God's interests will come into perfect harmony. God will begin to work IN the heart of the praying believer those things which are well-pleasing in His sight. (Philippians 2:13; Hebrews 13:20-21)

> But seek ye first the kingdom of God, and his righteousness; and all these things shall be added unto you. (Matthew 6:33)

Principles of Petitionary Prayer | **22**

Give us this day our daily bread. (Matthew 6:11)

This is a prayer of petition. In it, three areas of human need are dealt with:

1. *Physical* — "bread" — implies material needs.

2. *Mental* — "daily" — the implication is to live one day at a time. Don't worry about tomorrow. Worry is just as much a sin as swearing or cursing. (Read Matthew 6:25-34.)

3. *Spiritual* — "this day" — implies a daily contact with the Heavenly Father.

God is concerned about every area of our lives. He is interested not only in our spiritual well-being, but also our mental and physical well-being.

Beloved, I wish above all things that thou mayest prosper and be in health, even as thy soul prospereth. (3 John 1:2)

WHAT IS A PETITIONARY PRAYER?

A petitionary prayer is a personal request for the supply of a specific need or desire. There are rules or principles which are to be followed in petitionary-type prayer.

Principles of prayer are important, and not difficult to learn. Why are they important? It's just like anything else; do the right thing for the right results. When my daughter was two, she thought that no matter what number she dialed on the telephone she'd get grandma. But the only way she reached grandma was when the correct number was dialed. The principle: Dial the right number and you'll get the right party. In prayer, use the right principles and you'll get the right result. God understands when we are baby Christians we can't "dial the right number," so He overlooks our ignorance. But there comes a time we should learn to grow up, move onward and press toward maturity in prayer.

PRINCIPLES OF PETITIONARY PRAYER

1. *WE MUST RECOGNIZE OUR NEED.* This is true in salvation. If a person doesn't see his need for Jesus Christ, he will probably not ask for salvation. In the Alcoholic's Anonymous program, the first thing a person must do is admit that he is an alcoholic and in need of outside help. In becoming a Christian the first step a person must take is to recognize the fact that he is a sinner, away from God, and in need of a Savior.

   It is important when interceding for unsaved loved ones to pray that God will show them their need of Jesus.

   Why don't some people recognize their neediness? I think I have found essentially two related reasons.

   a. *Pride* — This is the "I've arrived" attitude. "I have need of nothing" (Revelation 3:15-17).

b. *Ungodly contentment* — People who are just satisfied to be alive, no dreams, no goals, no high aspirations — just content to be breathing.

There was an old guy who got up every morning to check the obituary column in the daily newspaper. If his name wasn't listed, he would breathe a sigh of relief and go back to bed.

Some folks are like that. They do nothing, go nowhere, and help nobody. Don't be like that! Don't be content to just be alive. Life is too short to be little. St. Paul said to "*press on*," not to "*sit back.*" Don't wait for your name to appear in the obituary column.

If you want to recognize your neediness of God, simply dream big dreams! Set big faith-goals beyond yourself so you'll have to look to God to meet the needs. It's important we recognize our neediness!

2. *RECOGNIZING THE FACT THAT GOD WANTS TO MEET OUR NEEDS.* The second step to powerful petitionary prayer is to understand that God actually DESIRES STRONGLY to give us good things!

> Ask, and it shall be given you; seek, and ye shall find; knock, and it shall be opened unto you: For every one that asketh receiveth; and he that seeketh findeth; and to him that knocketh it shall be opened. (Matthew 7:7-8)

God would not have said "ASK" if He didn't want us to receive. He would not have said "SEEK" if He didn't want us to find. He would never have told us to "KNOCK" if He didn't intend to open the door! God is a good God. Notice the first letter in each word: Ask, Seek, and Knock. It spells ASK.

We'll probably cry when we first get to heaven and find out all that we could have had if only we had dared to ASK.

> Ye have not because ye ASK not (James 4:2)

God urges us to come and ASK. He almost begs us to ASK. He delights in answering His children who are bold enough to ASK Him for good things. Not only does God want to supply our needs adequately, He wants to supply them ABUNDANTLY. But we have to ASK!

3. *REALIZE THAT WE CAN'T PURCHASE ANSWERED PRAYER.* This is the third principle of petitionary prayer: To realize that we can't buy answered prayer. Jesus said, "GIVE us this day our daily bread," not "SELL us this day our daily bread."

Answered prayer comes on the basis of faith alone, not the merit system. God is moved only by faith. (Hebrews 11:6) When a person needs something from God and enters prayer by reminding Him, "*Oh, I've been faithful to the church all these years and I've always paid my tithes, and I've taught Sunday School for ten years,*" he will get nowhere fast.

God is glad that you've attended church and paid your tithes "*all these years.*" That's an indication of your sincerity toward Him. But sincerity (as important as it is) does not get results from God. FAITH does!

What is faith?

> It is the confident assurance that something we want is going to happen. It is the certainty that what we hope for is waiting for us, even though we cannot see it up ahead. (Hebrews 11:1 TLB)

In other words, FAITH EXPECTS THE ANSWER!

[21] Jesus answered and said unto them, Verily I say unto you, If ye have faith and doubt not, ye shall not only do this which is done to the fig tree, but also if ye shall say unto this mountain, Be thou removed, and be thou cast into the sea; it shall be done.
[22] And all things, whatsoever ye shall ask in prayer, believing, ye shall receive. (Matthew 21:21-22)

A dear saintly woman read this Scripture before going to bed at night and got real brave. She decided that she was tired of that old mountain next door to her house, so she decided to *"pray it away."* She prayed, *"Oh Lord, please remove that mountain by tomorrow morning!"* When she awoke, the mountain was still there. She looked out the window and said, *"Just as I expected!"*

By contrast, a seven-year-old boy went to bed one night with a rope tied around his bedpost. His father came into the room and asked, *"Son, what is the rope for?"* *"Oh I prayed that the Lord would send me a pet donkey and I wanted to have something ready to tie him up with when he comes."*

Of course this is a comical illustration, but it does depict a valuable truth: When you pray, believe the answer is on the way. Call it DONE (Romans 4:17)!

4. *REALIZE THE UTTER NECESSITY OF DAILY CONTACT WITH GOD AND DAILY DEPENDENCE UPON GOD.* Jesus didn't tell us to pray, *"Give us this day our YEARLY bread."* He said to pray, *"Give us this day our DAILY bread."* God wants us to appreciate a daily dependence upon Him.

Most of us don't care to operate on such a small margin. We would much rather have a reserve to fall back on than to be in a place of absolute dependence upon the Lord. The children of Israel were examples of this. They were instructed to gather only enough manna for a day's supply, but some of them tried to store up more, just in case it failed to "rain" manna the next day. Did they get ahead? No. Their stockpile of manna bred worms and became unfit for human consumption.

God desires us to have a daily conference with Him. When a person's spiritual life begins to deteriorate, generally the cause can be traced to a lack of consistent daily prayer.

If ministers or other Christian workers fail to make daily prayer a business, the enemy will undoubtedly keep their efforts paralyzed.

VALUE OF DAILY PRAYER FOR PROTECTION

Here is an illustration of the value of daily prayer. I take the liberty to quote from Gordon Lindsay's best seller, *PRAYER THAT MOVES MOUNTAINS*:

"The importance of daily prayer, a daily meeting with God, and not just a casual saying of prayers is forcefully illustrated in the story of a Christian Armenian merchant who was carrying merchandise by caravan across the desert to a town in Turkish Armenia. Having been brought up by Christian parents he had formed a life habit of daily committing himself into the hands of God.

"At the time of this incident, the country was infested with "Kurds," that is bandits who lived by robbing caravans. Unknown to the merchant, a band of these highwaymen had been following the caravan, intending to rob it at the first camping place on the plains.

"At the chosen hour, under cover of darkness, they drew near. All was strangely quiet. There seemed to be no guards, no watchers but, as they pressed up, to their astonishment, they found high walls where walls had never stood before.

"They continued to follow but, the next night, they found the same impassable walls. The third night the walls stood but there were breaches in them through which they went in.

"The captain of the robbers, terrified by the mystery, awakened the merchant.

"'What does this mean?' said he. 'Ever since you left Ezerum, we have followed, intending to rob you. The first night and the second night we found high walls around the caravan but, tonight, we entered through broken places. If you will tell us the secret of all this, I will not molest you.'

"The merchant, himself, was surprised and puzzled. 'My friends,' he said, 'I have done nothing to have walls raised about us. All I do is pray every evening, committing myself and those with me to God. I fully trust in Him to keep me from all evil; but tonight, being very tired and sleepy, I made a rather half-hearted lip prayer. That must be why you were allowed to break through!'

"The Kurds were overcome by such testimony as this. Then and there, they gave themselves to Jesus Christ, and were saved. From caravan robbers, they became God fearing men. The Armenians, however, never forgot that breach in the wall of prayer."

5. REALIZE THAT PETITIONARY PRAYER MUST BE DEFINITE. The fifth principle of petitionary prayer is that the request must be specific.

By implication of principle, Jesus said, "*Give us this day our material needs.*" But by application of that principle, He narrowed it down to a specific, definite request for "*bread.*" It could have been *"milk"* or *"butter"* or *"meat,"* the point is, Jesus was specific.

Jesus encouraged us to pray for specific things and to expect God to answer.

> Therefore I say unto you, What things soever ye desire, when ye pray, believe that ye receive them and ye shall have them. (Mark 11:24)

One of the mistakes people make when they pray is that their praying is not specific. They ask for blessings, help, guidance — all of which are fine — except that their prayers aren't definite.

When you go to an earthly bank and need some money, you tell the clerk exactly what you want. When you go to your heavenly bank, you should do the same.

What is it that you need? Healing? Finances? Church growth? Write it out in vivid detail, ask God to fill your request and believe it's on the way. If the request is wrong, God will change your heart. Don't be afraid to ASK, BELIEVE, and PICTURE with your eye of faith, big things from God.

IN REVIEW — THE FIVE PRINCIPLES OF PETITIONARY PRAYER:

1. Recognize your need.
2. Recognize that God can and is willing to meet your needs.
3. Realize you can't buy answered prayer.
4. Realize the necessity of daily contact.
5. Realize that petitionary prayer must be specific.

Forgiveness: Key to Power | 23 |

> And forgive us our debts, as we forgive our debtors.
> (Matthew 6:12)

Forgiveness is the only subject in this model prayer that Jesus felt it necessary to amplify upon.

> [14] For if ye forgive men their trespasses, your heavenly Father will also forgive you:
> [15] But if ye forgive not men their trespasses, neither will your Father forgive your trespasses. (Matthew 6:14-15)

Forgiveness means the complete canceling of a debt. In other words, when one is forgiven, it is just as if he had never been a debtor or had never done anything wrong. Forgiveness is not merely, "I accept your apology." Forgiveness is a total healing and the cancellation of the debt.

The forgiveness we receive from God is in direct proportion to the forgiveness we offer to others (see also Mark 11:2-26).

A man approached John Wesley one day and said, "I'll never forgive!" Wesley responded, "Then you better pray that you never sin!"

HARMONY

Harmony is vital to a Christian family, association, or church. Jesus indicated that His presence would accompany harmonious Christian fellowship.

¹⁹ Again I say unto you, That if two of you shall agree on earth as touching any thing that they shall ask, it shall be done for them of my Father which is in heaven.

²⁰ For where two or three are gathered together in my name, there am I in the midst of them". (Matthew 18:19-20)

Harmony among believers brings the very presence of Jesus. The word "agree" actually means "spiritual harmony" or "symphony." So when we gather together in agreement and in the name of Jesus, we can fully expect the presence of our Lord. And if He is there, we can rest assured that miracles will occur!

On the other hand, strife (or disharmony) will bring another presence. James 3:16 says that where "strife is, there is confusion and every evil work." Disharmony actually brings the presence of evil into a situation.

I have seen, on rare occasions, people who sat in our meetings whose faces radiated a countenance of evil. It was like radar — you could just tell they weren't in harmony with the others. They were unwittingly taken captive by the devil. (II Timothy 2:24-26)

There are two choices in relationships: HARMONY or STRIFE. Harmony brings the presence of Jesus among Christians; disharmony brings the presence of evil. Too many Christians try to do the work of God while in the presence of evil. That is why they are left to struggle in their failures.

The Bible is clear on the matter. If a person is causing disharmony among a body of believers, the first approach is restoration through repentance and FORGIVENESS. If that fails, he is to be cast out.

If he neglects to hear the church, let him be unto thee as an heathen man and a publican. (Matthew 18:17)

If anyone is causing divisions among you, he should be given a first and second warning. After that have nothing more to do with him. (Titus 3:10 TLB)

Mark them which cause division ... and avoid them. (Romans 16:17)

God tells us the things that cause disharmony and strife in a church and tells us they will hinder church growth. A person involved in these things is hindering the Kingdom of God, not helping the Kingdom of God.

ENEMIES OF CHURCH GROWTH
(2 Corinthians 12:20-21 NIV)

1. Quarreling
2. Jealousy
3. Outbursts of anger
4. Factions
5. Slander
6. Gossip
7. Arrogance
8. Disorder
9. Unrepented sin
10. Debauchery

Harmony is vital to the growth, expansion and development of any Christian endeavor.

If you keep on biting and devouring each other, watch out or you will be destroyed by each other. (Galatians 5:15)

LEADING EVANGELIST

Years ago, one of the nation's leading evangelists, discovered that some of his staff members were murmuring and complaining about things they didn't understand. They were guilty of the same sin as the children of Israel.

> And do not grumble, as some of them did —and were killed by the destroying angel. (1 Corinthians 10:10 NIV)

So the evangelist called a staff meeting. He said essentially this:

> "Listen, The Word of God indicates to us that if we operate in harmony, we will be assured of the presence of Jesus. The Bible tells us, however, that the person causing strife or disharmony will be influenced and controlled by confusion and evil! (2 Timothy 2:24-26; James 3:16) From this day forth there will be no disharmony in this ministry. If I find out about anyone complaining or grumbling, or 'bucking the program,' they'll have a short time to repent and will be forgiven. But if it continues, they will be fired on-the-spot. We will still forgive them and help them find another job somewhere, but they will not function in this ministry again. I believe harmony in this ministry is important."

Well, they all made a commitment to harmony. Like never before, opportunities arose to complain and grumble. The testing came, but they were now committed! It became fun pushing for harmony; a real challenge. Nobody wanted to be the one to break the unity and the awareness of Jesus' presence in that ministry. What was the result? In less than 90 days the ministry income and outreach doubled! The overall ministry and effectiveness doubled in less than three months.

Oh, how easy it would be to work in God's Kingdom with a constant awareness of Jesus' presence. But how difficult it can be when one or two people decide to be in disharmony, thereby attracting an evil presence like a magnet attracts steel.

WHY IS HARMONY DIFFICULT?

Harmony is difficult because we are dealing with imperfect human beings. From a theological standpoint, every believer is "perfect" in God's eyes because of our obedience to the Gospel of Jesus. But from an experiential standpoint (a practical point of view), we are still people who don't always do the right thing. That's why you can't find a perfect church. You can hop all over town, attending every church and fellowship and never find the "perfect group." That's because every church is made up of people like you and me; people who sometimes think things we shouldn't, and say things we shouldn't, and do things we shouldn't.

Churches are made up of people who need forgiveness from God, and from each other.

What is the key to harmony and power with God? FORGIVENESS. Not just, "I accept your apology," but a total healing. That's the *best way*.

Forgiveness — *Continued* | **24**

This chapter will require the reading of the *Parable of the Unmerciful Servant*.

²³ Therefore is the kingdom of heaven likened unto a certain king, which would take account of his servants.

²⁴ And when he had begun to reckon, one was brought unto him, which owed him ten thousand talents.

²⁵ But forasmuch as he had not to pay, his lord commanded him to be sold, and his wife, and children, and all that he had, and payment to be made.

²⁶ The servant therefore fell down, and worshipped him saying, Lord, have patience with me, and I will pay thee all.

²⁷ Then the lord of that servant was moved with compassion, and loosed him, and forgave him the debt.

²⁸ But the same servant went out, and found one of his fellowservants, which owed him an hundred pence: and he laid hands on him, and took him by the throat saying, Pay me that thou owest.

²⁹ And his fellowservant fell down at his feet, and besought him saying, Have patience with me, and I will pay thee all.

³⁰ And he would not: but went and cast him into prison till he should pay the debt.

³¹ So when his fellowservants saw what was done, they were very sorry, and came and told unto their lord all that was done.

³² Then his lord, after that he had called him, said unto him, O thou wicked servant, I forgave thee all that debt, because thou desiredst me:

³³ Shouldest not thou also have had compassion on thy fellowservant, even as I had pity on thee?

³⁴ And his lord was wroth, and delivered him to the tormentors, till he should pay all that was due unto him.

³⁵ So likewise shall my heavenly Father do also unto you, if ye from your hearts forgive not every one his brother their trespasses. (Matthew 18:23-35)

Ten thousand talents equal about $12 million. One hundred pence equals about $15.00.

The unmerciful servant was forgiven — his huge debts were completely canceled—but he wouldn't forgive his fellowservant who owed him a measly $15.00. The result? Torment! (Verse 34)

When we don't forgive, we are turned over to the hands of evil tormentors. What kind of torment do we experience when we don't forgive?

1 - SPIRITUAL TORMENT

It is tormenting to try to pray with the gnawing suspicion that you are not completely clean before God. That torment comes from unforgiveness. Jesus said, "If you desire forgiveness, you must forgive."

Almost every where I go, I see people rebuking the devil, binding the devil and "breaking the power" of the devil. But when unforgiveness prevails, you can "rebuke, bind and break" until your voice box goes numb, but you'll still be trapped in spiritual torment! Matthew 18:34 leaves nothing to be misunderstood. If the Father, Himself, allows you to be in a spiritual prison, there can be no freedom until the right conditions are met. In this case, the right condition is forgiveness.

Another tormenting situation is a lack of direction. God reveals to us in His Word that if we hate our brother, we walk in darkness. (1 John 2:9) Unforgiveness is a form of hatred, and darkness is the opposite of light. Therefore, when we don't forgive others their wrong, we'll not receive divine guidance or direction in our lives. That's torment!

2 - MENTAL TORMENT

Mental torment comes to the person who holds resentment and grudges. For the grudge holder there is no genuine, lasting joy or peace. Instead his life seems to be in constant turmoil. Symptoms of unforgiveness may vary, but you can be sure that the unforgiving person will experience periods of deep depression and gloominess. He may feel rejected, fearful or insecure and will probably develop a critical attitude.

A pastor's wife once lived in torment because she held grudges against people who had borrowed tapes and books, but never returned them to her. One day, her husband preached a message on forgiveness and a scripture came to her mind. "Lend, expecting nothing in return." With that thought in mind she said, "Father, I forgive them." Then she named all the people she held resentment toward. Instantly she was released from the tormentor! By the next week, people began returning her tapes and books, as if they had been divinely reminded!

Forgiveness brings a release from the tormentor!

3 - PHYSICAL TORMENT

Medical science has proven beyond question that unforgiveness, resentment and grudges all cause problems in your physical health.

A Viet Nam Veteran was very bitter toward the U.S. Government for sending him to war. In Viet Nam, he stepped on a mine, lost his hearing, and developed other physical problems. His condition only grew worse as he verbalized his bitterness.

One night he attended a church service where forgiveness was preached. Afterward, he broke down and said, "I forgive the U.S. Government." When he did, his ears were healed and his other problems began to mend that very moment!

Think of unforgiveness as an unwanted wart growing in your body. Perhaps your brain, or your heart; maybe your kidneys. That's what unforgiveness is — a root — an unwanted root of bitterness that can cause all manner of physical affliction.

I know of a minister who taught on the subject of forgiveness in a special meeting. When he led the people in a prayer of forgiveness for others to whom they were holding resentments, suddenly, people began to be healed of physical problems! Forgiveness and good health are very much related.

What is the way of release from the tormentor? FORGIVENESS!

[25] And when ye stand praying, forgive, if ye have ought against any: that your Father also which is in heaven may forgive you your trespasses.
[26] But if ye do not forgive, neither will your Father which is in heaven forgive your trespasses. (Mark 11:25-26)

How to Forgive | 25

Let's look back at the Parable of the Unmerciful Servant. In verse 32 (Matt. 18), he is addressed as a "wicked servant." Why do you suppose Jesus called him "*wicked*?" Because he failed to forgive after he, himself, had just been forgiven 800,000 times more than what was owed him.

Christians are to be ministers of reconciliation, not condemnation.

> [18] And all things are of God, who hath reconciled us to himself by Jesus Christ, and hath given to us the ministry of reconciliation;
>
> [19] To wit, that God was in Christ, reconciling the world unto himself, not imputing their trespasses unto them; and hath committed us to the word of reconciliation. (2 Corinthians 5:18-19)

> [16] For God so loved the world, that he gave his only begotten Son, that whosoever believeth in him should not perish, but have everlasting life.
>
> [17] For God sent not his Son into the world to condemn the world; but that the world through him might be saved" (John 3:16-17).

Look at John 20:23:

> Whosoever's sins ye remit, they are remitted unto them, and whosoever's sins ye retain, they are retained.

Did you know that you, as a Christian, have the power to keep people retained in their sins? You can keep people bound in their sins by invisible chains of unforgiveness. Matthew 18:30 verifies this truth. Some people keep their unsaved loved ones in spiritual chains because they won't forgive them of past debts and wrongs.

I read about an older couple who accepted Christ later in life, after their children were already grown. This couple had developed a resentment toward their oldest son. He was involved in a motorcycle gang, and every time they saw him, it seemed like he had moved another step further in the wrong direction. They resented his life-style and it showed. One day, after learning the spiritual principles involved in forgiveness, they both forgave their son all his wrong doing. When they did, they actually released him from a spiritual prison. In two weeks' time, he repented of his ways and accepted Christ as his Savior.

It's not an easy matter to forgive. But it's necessary! If we desire the abundant life of which Jesus spoke, our only option is to forgive.

HOW TO FORGIVE

1. *ADMIT YOUR OWN DEBTS.* Stop and think about all the slanders, covetousness, gluttony, and envy God has forgiven in you. You never could have paid your debt to God if Jesus hadn't completely canceled it for you.

2. *CONFESS ALL UNFORGIVENESS AS SIN.* (1 John 1:9)

3. *FORGIVE AS AN ACT OF FAITH, NOT FEELINGS!* You will not feel like forgiving. You will want to hold a grudge. That's why you must firmly *decide* to forgive, not by what you feel, but because God instructs you to forgive.

Who do you need to forgive? An aunt? An uncle? A parent? A child? A teacher? A brother? A sister? An employer? An ex-wife? An ex-husband? A minister? Someone who is dead?

Corrie Ten Boom didn't *feel* like forgiving the concentration camp guard who not only kept her confined, but was partly responsible for her sister's death. She didn't want to, but when confronted with that guard, she whispered the prayer, "Jesus, please forgive this person through me for I am weak." It worked *NOT by feelings but by faith*.

Goldie Bristol didn't forgive the man who molested and killed her daughter because of her feelings for him. It was hard to do, but she forgave him, and even visited him in prison, because of her faith in Jesus.

Forgiveness is not an easy assignment. But in order to be forgiven, we must forgive.

4. SAY IT: "I FORGIVE ___(name them)___ ."

5. NEVER TALK RESENTFULLY ABOUT THE OLD HURT AGAIN. NEVER TALK RESENTFULLY ABOUT THE PERSON YOU'VE FORGIVEN.

Talking about a hurt in a resentful manner is like fertilizing the wart of unforgiveness. It feeds on your words and grows bigger as you vocalize your bitterness. Give up grudges like you'd give up cancer.

Forgiveness is *the* key to harmony, unity, deliverance and healing! Forgiveness is *a* key to POWER WITH GOD.

Avoiding Evil | **26**

And lead us not into temptation, but deliver us from evil; For thine is the kingdom, and the power, and the glory, for ever. Amen. (Matthew 6:13)

That verse can be broken down into three sections:

1. DON'T (lead us into temptation)
2. DO (deliver us from evil)
3. BENEDICTION

WHAT IS A TEMPTATION?

A temptation is an allurement, inducement, or attraction to ANYTHING outside of God's perfect will. It will usually involve selfishness, ambition or pride. All of us have faced temptations.

In Jesus' model prayer, the phrase "lead us not into temptation" has a dual application. First, it involves praying against personal temptations that may eventually be experienced. Secondly, it likely refers to the deliverance from the coming hour of temptation this whole world will face in the future. (Revelation 3:10)

All of us meet personal temptations almost daily. These temptations range anywhere from taking an extra 15 minutes for coffee break to the deepest form of immorality imaginable. I know a Christian who was actually tempted to murder his wife! That's hard for most people to imagine. The likelihood is slim that all of us have been tempted to murder. But all of us have met other temptations head on!

The point is this: Temptations come, and each is custom made. The devil studies your strong points and your weak points. He scrutinizes you with a fine-tooth comb, then he sets customized traps for you in the form of temptations. As hunters use different traps for different animals, so the devil sets unique traps for various people.

There are, however, some subtle temptations that are common to all Christians. Paul listed them in Galatians 5:26:

> Let us not be desirous of vainglory, provoking one another, envying one another.

1. DESIRING HONOR FOR YOURSELF. This may be demonstrated by promoting yourself for the lead role in a church play. Or perhaps you may be tempted to pray extra loud so people will think you are a great prayer warrior. This is such a sneaky temptation it is often hard to catch.

2. PROVOKING ONE ANOTHER. This has a dual meaning in the original languages. It means: 1) irritating one another, and 2) comparing yourself with one another.

3. ENVYING ONE ANOTHER. "I don't know why the Joneses drive a Cadillac and we don't!"

Temptations are custom made to fit the situation and to fit the individual.

SEVEN STAGES IN A PERSONAL TEMPTATION

There are seven stages in a personal temptation:

1. The thought comes. (This is not sin.)
2. The imagination gains strength.
3. You begin to delight in viewing the thought (this is the bridge between the original thought and actual sin).
4. The will begins to weaken.
5. Yielding occurs.
6. You commit the sinful act.
7. The penalty must be paid: death — separation from the awareness of God's presence.

Jesus said, "Watch and pray, that ye enter not into temptation." (Matthew 26:41)

That means, when you face a temptation, if you are watching, and if you are praying, you will not enter into the POWER of temptation. Jesus has been through every form of temptation, and is well able to pull us out when we are tempted.

> For in that he himself hath suffered being tempted, he is able to succour them that are tempted. (Hebrews 2:18)

In a local factory there is a sign next to a conveyor belt that reads, "IN CASE OF TROUBLE, CALL THE MANAGER." Every employee knows the standard rule in case of trouble is to call the manager FIRST!

One day, as the conveyor belt moved on, one of the worker's sleeves got caught in the belt. She reasoned, *Oh, I can get it out.* She tried to free the sleeve, but could not. So the conveyor and the employee kept moving along. Each tug of the conveyor made the woman feel more silly and eventually she was too embarrassed to yell for help. She tugged. She struggled. She tried to get free, but she could not loosen her sleeve from that belt. Then, just as she was about to be dragged into a dangerous piece of machinery, her arm tripped the safety switch. The conveyor belt stopped, and so did everything else. The entire factory completely shut down. Very quickly, the manager came and asked, "What happened?"

The factory worker nervously replied, "I got my sleeve tangled up in the conveyor belt. I did everything I could to get it out."

"No, you didn't," steamed the manager as he pointed to the sign. "You never called the manager. Now it's going to take over four hours to get all this equipment up and running again!"

Are you staring a temptation in the face? Don't take a chance on "shutting the system down." Your own feeble efforts are not powerful enough to free you from the "conveyor belt" of temptation. CALL THE MANAGER! His name is Jesus.

ANOTHER APPLICATION

The second application of "LEAD US NOT INTO TEMPTATION," is for the Church at large. Many Bible authorities believe Jesus was teaching us to pray that we will not be led into the HOUR OF TEMPTATION which is coming to the entire earth.

In Revelation 3:10, Jesus promises a certain segment of Christianity will escape the coming terror of the Great Tribulation (hour of temptation).

> Because thou hast kept the word of my patience, I also will keep thee from the hour of temptation, which shall come upon all the world, to try them that dwell upon the earth. (Revelation 3:10)

Also, Jesus tells us to pray that we will escape all the terrible hardships He spoke of when describing the earth's final three and one-half years of bloodshed and terror.

> [35] For as a snare shall it come on all them that dwell on the face of the whole earth.
> [36] Watch ye therefore, and pray always, that ye may be accounted worthy to escape all these things that shall come to pass, and to stand before the Son of man. (Luke 21:35-36)

Apparently, those who are praying for deliverance will be snatched from the earth just prior to the rise of Antichrist. What a glorious time that will be!

DELIVER US FROM EVIL

A common complaint among many people is, "Why did this happen to me?" Some people pray only after tragedy overtakes them, not seeming to realize that had they prayed sooner, they might have avoided the disaster.

At this moment, Satan is busy setting snares to make your life miserable. He's on duty 24 hours a day. He doesn't sleep. And half-hearted, self-centered prayers are not adequate to thwart the enemy and avoid disaster. The devil sets some very attractive snares. Without discernment and spiritual power, they are difficult to overcome.

If before World War II the Christians in Germany were praying, "Deliver us from evil," the holocaust may never have taken place. The Christians had it in their grasp to change the course of history, but instead they were deceived. Adolf Hitler came along, carrying his Bible and promising to restore morality and decency to the nation. Many Christians who were not praying for deliverance from evil thought, *This is our man*. Hitler became the nation's leader and, alas, it was too late!

Through prayer and faith, we can come to a place of protection and safety. We can actually anticipate evil and be delivered from it before it can reach us.

> My enemies have set a trap for me. Frantic fear grips me. They have dug a pitfall in my path. But look! They themselves have fallen into it! (Psalm 57:6 TLB)

I imagine the devil and his demons setting snares for my life, family, and ministry. Then I pray, "Father, wherever the devil is setting traps for me, please send angels ahead of me to spring those traps on the devil and his workers." Can't you just see it? Demons and their partners caught in the snares they were setting for me! And now that they're trapped, all I do is walk by, surrounded by the promises of God, and think, *It serves you right, devil!*

Study Psalm 91 and seize God's promises for your life.

FOR THINE IS THE KINGDOM
AND THE POWER,
AND THE GLORY,
FOREVER, AMEN!

Christian Meditation | 27

Do you want the Holy Spirit to speak to you, direct you, and make the promises in God's Word come alive in your life? Christian meditation is one method by which the Holy Spirit can operate to do just that.

Meditation is Biblical. In fact, the Bible frequently tells us that meditation is a necessary step to success. For example:

1. Joshua 1:8 - meditation leads to success and prosperity.
2. Psalm 1:1-3 - meditation is a key to prosperity.
3. 1 Timothy 4:15 - meditation leads to profiting.

Do you want to profit? Do you desire success? Do you want to be prosperous? If so, you must learn the art of meditation.

As you learn how to meditate upon God's Word, you'll find yourself getting to the place where you will supernaturally know things in your spirit. Supernatural perception for various situations will flourish and faith will come alive in your heart.

Meditating on God's Word is digesting spiritual food.

Reading and hearing the Word is similar to putting food in your mouth. Studying the Word is like chewing your food.

But meditating upon the Word is like digesting the food; it becomes a part of you.

WHAT CHRISTIAN MEDITATION IS NOT

1. *IT IS NOT OCCULTISM.* It is not transcendental meditation or any other Eastern religious practices.

2. *IT IS NOT DAYDREAMING.* Daydreams are unreal, impractical, irrational, purposeless fantasies. "If I had a million dollars, I would ...." Thinking like this is counter-productive.

3. *IT IS NOT SPIRITUALIZING THE SCRIPTURES.* In other words, meditation does not mean to get some strange mystical, hidden meaning from the Scriptures.

WHAT CHRISTIAN MEDITATION IS

Christian meditation means "waiting upon the Word of God which is on the outside of me, until it is explained to me by the Holy Spirit, who is on the inside of me." It involves pondering, reflecting, and examining a Scripture or a Promise from all angles.

The disciples often asked Jesus questions concerning His teachings. They would get alone with Him, and He would explain things to them. In meditation, we ask God questions about His Word, then wait for Him to open our understanding.

> [9] But as it is written, Eye hath not seen, nor ear heard, neither have entered into the heart of man, the things which God hath prepared for them that love him.
> [10] But God hath revealed them unto us by his Spirit: for the Spirit searcheth all things, yea, the deep things of God. (1 Corinthians 2:9-10)

But the comforter, which is the Holy Ghost, whom the Father will send in my name, he shall teach you all things, and bring all things to your remembrance, whatsoever I have said unto you. (John 14:26)

Then opened he their understanding, that they might understand the scriptures. (Luke 24:25)

Isaac went to the fields to meditate. Joseph was meditating when an angel appeared to him.

HOW TO PRACTICE CHRISTIAN MEDITATION

Do you want to learn the art of meditation? This is how it's done:

1. *Take a Scripture or a portion of Scripture, or take one promise from the Bible.* (It's important to take just one to start with.)

2. *Read it.*

3. *Re-read it.*

4. *Think about it.*

5. *View it from all angles.* Take a journalistic approach by asking: Who? What? Where? When? Why? How?

6. *Ask God questions concerning that Scripture.*

7. *Read it over and over again.* Speak it with your mouth. Think about it all day; when you get up and when you go to bed.

As you do this, you'll be aware of the faith rising in your spirit. You will receive revelation knowledge from the Holy

Spirit. You will experience an assurance of God's willingness and ability to keep His Word.

I know of a young lady who was barren by medical standards. Her doctors said she'd never be able to have children. She went home, took her Bible and found a Scripture in Exodus that promises God's people fertility. She meditated upon it. Soon God led her to another Scripture in Deuteronomy that promises no barrenness for the children of God. Then she found an amazing promise in Mark 11:24:

> Therefore I say unto you, what things soever ye desire, when ye pray, believe that ye receive them, and ye shall have them.

She certainly desired a child so she prayed. She meditated upon God's promises day and night, and soon faith poured into her heart. She put her faith in God, now she has two fine children of her own! Her testimony is proof of the power of Christian Meditation.

WRONG MEDITATION

David said, "May the words of my mouth and the meditations of my heart be pleasing in your sight." (Psalm 19:14) It is possible to have wrong meditations that are not pleasing to God. Here are five of them:

1. *Worry*
2. *Evil Imaginations*
3. *Reviewing Hurts*
4. *Reviewing Failures*
5. *Meditating outside the boundaries of God's Word*

A PLAN OF ACTION

Take one promise from the Bible and talk about it all week. Meditate upon it. Use the seven steps I shared with you, then watch your faith come alive. You will develop a "KNOWING" that you are going to be successful.

God will reveal things to your heart like never before!

The Spiritual Language | 28

We have learned the value of Bible meditation and have seen how God speaks to us through this exercise. Now, let's look at another new dimension of prayer we can experience with God.

> [26] Likewise the Spirit also helpeth our infirmities: for we know not what we should pray for as we ought: but the Spirit itself maketh intercession for us with groanings which cannot be uttered.
> [27] And he that searcheth the hearts knoweth what is the mind of the Spirit, because he maketh intercession for the saints according to the will of God. (Romans 8:26, 27)

> Praying always with all prayer and supplication IN THE SPIRIT, and watching thereunto with all perseverance and supplication for all saints. (Ephesians 6:18)

> But ye, beloved, building up yourselves on your most holy faith, praying IN THE HOLY GHOST. (Jude 20)

> What is it then? I will pray WITH THE SPIRIT, and I will pray with the understanding also: I will sing WITH THE SPIRIT, and I will sing with the understanding also. (1 Corinthians 14:15)

WHAT DOES "IN THE SPIRIT" OR "WITH THE SPIRIT" ACTUALLY MEAN?

It's important to let the Scripture interpret the Scripture.

> ...comparing spiritual things with spiritual. (1 Corinthians 2:13)

> For he that speaketh in an *unknown* tongue speaketh not unto men, but unto God: for no man understandeth him, howbeit in the spirit he speaketh mysteries. (1 Corinthians 14:2)

Notice: A person speaking IN THE SPIRIT is speaking "mysteries." In other words, he is speaking something that is a mystery to his own intellect, but not a mystery to God.

> What is it then? I will pray with the spirit, and I will pray with the understanding also: I will sing with the spirit, and I will sing with the understanding also. (1 Corinthians 14:15)

Notice: Paul says to pray two different ways. Number one —"WITH THE SPIRIT." Number two — "WITH THE UNDERSTANDING." It is clear that when one prays with the Spirit, he is praying without his mental understanding.

In the Greek language, the practice of praying or speaking "IN THE SPIRIT" is called *glossolalia*, which means "speaking in languages never learned by the speaker." In other words, it means to pray in a language you don't mentally understand. It is a supernatural impartation of the Holy Spirit. That means it is part "super" and part "natural." The concept of GOD working WITH man once again is clear.

This language is called by different names. Here are a few of the names for this unknown language:

- Prayer Language
- Heavenly Language
- Angelic Language
- Tongues
- Spiritual Language
- Glossolalia
- Unknown Tongues

It happened on the Day of Pentecost! When the Holy Spirit filled the believers, they began to praise God in a new spiritual language; one they had never learned. It's happening again today!

We are in the midst of a great, perhaps final, outpouring of the Holy Spirit. Christians from all cultures and denominations are beginning to receive this new prayer language, just as the early disciples received. They are discovering the pricelessness of the prayer language in prayer and in worship of our Lord Jesus.

As you study the New Testament and Church history, you'll discover that "speaking in tongues" (spiritual language) was considered normal Christianity.

> And they were all filled with the Holy Ghost, and began to speak with other tongues, as the Spirit gave them utterance. (Acts 2:4)

> 44 While Peter yet spake these words, the Holy Ghost fell on all them which heard the word.
> 45 And they of the circumcision which believed were astonished, as many as came with Peter, because that on the Gentiles also was poured out the gift of the Holy Ghost.
> 46 For they heard them speak with tongues, and magnify God. (Acts 10:44-46)

> And when Paul had laid his hands upon them, the Holy Ghost came on them, and they spake with tongues, and prophesied. (Acts 19:6)

St. Paul said, "I thank my God, I speak with tongues more than ye all." (1 Corinthians 14:18)

St. Augustine, the noted theologian and author of the famous *City of God* wrote:

> We still do what the apostles did when they laid hands on the Samaritans and called down the Holy Spirit on them by laying on of hands. It is expected that converts should speak with new tongues.

In *HISTORY OF THE CHRISTIAN CHURCH* by Philip Schaff, the author gave a considerable record of the speaking in other tongues in various revivals over a period of many centuries.

The *Encyclopedia Britannica* states that the glossolalia (or speaking in tongues) recurs in Christian revivals of every age, e.g. among Mendicant Friars of the 13th century, among the Jansenists and early Quakers, the persecuted Protestants of the Cevennes, and the Irvingites" (Vol. 17, pages 9, 10, Eleventh Edition).

Souer, in his German work entitled *HISTORY OF THE CHRISTIAN CHURCH* (Vol. 3, page 406), states that Martin Luther spoke in tongues!

Dr. A.B. Simpson, the founder of the Christian Missionary Alliance, made this report toward the close of his life when that great Pentecostal outpouring came:

> We believe there can be no doubt that in many cases remarkable outpourings of the Holy Spirit have been accomplished with genuine instances of the gift of tongues and many extraordinary manifestations. This has occurred both in our own land and in some of our foreign missions. Many of these experiences appear not only to be genuine, but accompanied by a spirit of deep humility and soberness, and free from extravagance and error. And it is admitted that in many of the branches and States where this movement has been strongly developed and wisely directed,there has been a marked deepening of the spiritual life of our members, and an encouraging increase in their missionary zeal and liberality. It would therefore be a serious matter for any candid Christian to pass a wholesale criticism or condemnation upon such movements, or presume to limit the Holy One of Israel.

You see, the practice of praying in a spiritual language is genuine. It appears that the only critics are those who are unscholarly, or dishonest, or just plain backslidden!

Churches which do not forbid their members to pray in tongues (1 Corinthians 14:39) are growing today by leaps and bounds. The power of God is there!

WHAT IS THE PURPOSE OF THE SPIRITUAL LANGUAGE?

1. *IT SHIFTS OUR EMPHASIS FROM MENTAL TO SPIRITUAL.*
God made man as a trichotomy; a spirit with a mind and
body. He intended that the spirit be in charge of the other
areas. However, we have made a god out of the intellect — the
mind. But the intellect can't bring satisfaction because we are
not primarily mental creatures. We are primarily spiritual
creatures.

Baal was the god of the intellect. He was the god of "mind
power!" Whenever we make plans, programs or decisions
based *solely* upon human reasoning and human logic, we
have unwittingly become Baal worshippers.

Some people won't turn their lives over to Jesus Christ
because they don't understand Him; they can't figure Him
out. Some won't believe because they can't understand how
Jesus can forgive them. You see, their god is Baal — the god
of mental understanding, intellect, the mind.

But God wants us to act primarily by spirit, not mind.
God's words are "*spirit*." (John 6:63) When we act upon God's
words, regardless of whether or not we fully understand
them, we are operating by spirit instead of by mind!

Jesus told 500 Christians to wait in Jerusalem for the
Promise of the Father (the power of the Holy Spirit). He told
them to wait! He didn't tell them to try to evangelize the
world first. He said to wait! Apparently 380 of them used

their human reasoning and logic instead of operating by the Spirit because they never showed up for the ten-day Jerusalem wait! Only 120 bothered to wait in Jerusalem for the power of the Holy Spirit. And that 120 went forth and turned the world upside down for Christ. The other 380 were never mentioned again. I wonder what happened to them? What was their effect on the world?

God's work *must* be accomplished in the Spirit! The prayer language helps put the Spirit at the top.

We Christians must operate by the Spirit, in the Spirit, with the Spirit and through the Spirit. Human reasoning and logic alone are not good enough for decision making, plan making, and program designing.

2. *THE PRAYER LANGUAGE, BEING OF THE SPIRIT, MAKES US AWARE OF THE FATHER'S PRESENCE AND CHARGES US WITH POWER!*

> For through him we both have access by one Spirit unto the Father. (Ephesians 2:18)

At our intercessory prayer meetings, we all praise God in our spiritual language. We bless with the Spirit (1 Corinthians 14:16), we sing in the Spirit (1 Corinthians 14:15; Colossians 3:16; Ephesians 5:17-19), and we wait upon the Father in praise.

There is such an awesome awareness of God's presence! He often speaks to us through prophecies or words of knowledge, as this offering of praise and thanksgiving goes before Him. God's heart is blessed and we are encouraged, comforted, strengthened and edified!

> He that speaketh in an unknown tongue edifieth himself.
> (1 Corinthians 14:4a.)

144

The word *edify* means to *charge up*. Using your spiritual language will charge you up! You may not feel the power but, you will know it's there by its results!

3. *THE SPIRITUAL LANGUAGE MAKES US HUMBLE.* (Mark 10:15-16) It's a humbling experience to speak in a silly-sounding language (that is, silly-sounding to our educated minds). But God understands and wants us to trust Him in childlike faith to speak forth these perfect prayers and praises.

4. *THE SPIRITUAL LANGUAGE HELPS US TO PRAISE, WORSHIP, AND THANK GOD IN A NEW DIMENSION.* (1 Corinthians 14:16-17; John 4:23-24) Have you ever wanted to say "Thanks, Lord," but couldn't find enough words, or the right words to express your appreciation to God? Well, the prayer language solves this problem perfectly.

5. *THE SPIRITUAL LANGUAGE HELPS OUR PRAYER INADEQUACIES.* (Romans 8:26-27) A skeptical, cocky army private came to the chaplain one day and said, "I'll believe in God if He'll answer a prayer. Ask your God to make me quit smoking." The chaplain laid his hands on the soldier and began to pray in the spiritual language. Then an interpretation came to him concerning the mysteries he was speaking in tongues. Without hardly thinking, he opened his mouth and said, "God don't let him smoke again as long as he lives!"

Several days later the cocky private came to the chaplain with a new enthusiasm. But he wasn't so cocky anymore! He had tried to smoke so he could prove that God doesn't answer prayer, but when he lit it up, he began vomiting! This same thing occurred for the next three days. Within minutes after telling the chaplain his story, the private dropped to his knees and accepted Jesus Christ as Lord and Savior!

I hope you can see the value of developing the spiritual language. It's a gift from the Holy Spirit to Christians who will ask God to fill them with the Holy Spirit. (Luke 11:13)

If you will do the *natural*, God will do the *super* and you'll have a supernatural new prayer language. Begin to praise God, but don't use English. Remember, it's *you* who speaks in tongues, not the Holy Spirit. He gives you the ability, but *you* must do it.

In the next chapter you'll learn how to advance even further in your life of prayer.

Interpreting Your Spiritual Language | 29 |

We now come to another exciting facet of our prayer life: Interpreting our Spiritual Language. That's right! God instructs those of us who speak in the prayer language to pray that we may interpret it also. This is not only for people who exercise the *gift* of tongues or interpretation in a church service, but for every Spirit-filled believer! If it were not so, God would not have said to pray that you may interpret.

> Wherefore let him that speaketh in an unknown tongue pray that he may interpret. (1 Corinthians 14:13)

I have discovered the *BEST* use of tongues and interpretation is in my private devotions. This is not to imply that the exclusive use of these gifts is reserved for personal prayer, however a careful study of 1 Corinthians, Chapter 14, will reveal that private devotions is a BETTER place for tongues and interpretation than the large corporate services.

> [18] I thank my God, I speak with tongues more than ye all:
> [19] Yet in the church I had rather speak five words with my understanding, that by my voice I might teach others also, than ten thousand words in an *unknown* tongue.
> [20] Brethren be not children in understanding: howbeit in malice be ye children, but in understanding be men. (1 Corinthians 14:18-20)

WHAT WILL THE INTERPRETATION CONTAIN?

There are approximately five possibilities regarding the content of an interpretation to your spiritual language. The interpretation may involve any one of these five components, or any combination of the five.

1. *PRAISE, BLESSINGS, WORSHIP, PRAYER, INTERCESSIONS OR THANKSGIVING*

The interpretation to your spiritual languages may involve some form of prayer or praise to the Father. Often we have difficulty finding the right words to say to God. Sometimes we don't know how to pray as we ought. But the Holy Spirit will help us through our prayer language.

Read:

Romans 8: 26-27
Acts 10:46
1 Corinthians 14:16-17

The Bible does not record one case of anyone preaching the Gospel in their spiritual language, although this is not impossible. The main use of this gift was to bless and magnify God.

2. *REVELATION*

The second thing an interpretation may involve is a revelation. A revelation is an act of making known something that has been a secret.

> ...howbeit, in the spirit he speaketh mysteries.
> (1 Corinthians 14:2)

> Now, brethren, if I come unto you speaking with tongues,
> what shall I profit you, except I shall speak to you either by
> REVELATION or by KNOWLEDGE, or by PROPHESYING, or by
> DOCTRINE? (1 Corinthians 14:6)

Years ago I learned the benefit of using my spiritual
language and interpreting it. I came home from work with an
awful feeling of guilt, or worry, or anxiety. Actually I couldn't
put my finger on what was bothering me. I tried praying. I
tried making a faith announcement of deliverance from this
uneasy feeling, but to no avail. Then I began to use my
spiritual language. At first my understanding was unfruitful,
but as I got quiet before the Lord, I asked Him to give me an
interpretation of the things I had uttered. Suddenly an idea
came to me out of my inner being. I followed it and spoke it
forth. Praise God! It was a REVELATION of what my problem
really was, and the solution to it!

3. *KNOWLEDGE*

An interpretation may be a supernatural impartation of
knowledge or facts which at the moment you have no way of
learning by natural means.

Merlin Carothers, a Methodist minister, was asked to give
the benediction in a Presbyterian Church he was visiting. He
walked to the platform, and instead of giving a regular
benediction, he called people to come forward to dedicate
their lives to Christ. People stood around the altars as Merlin
prayed over them in his prayer language. As interpretations
came to his spirit, Merlin spoke them forth. "Lord, forgive
this man for his drunkenness." "Lord, forgive this person for
dishonesty in business." "Please, Father, forgive this one for
robbing You by not paying tithes." Chaplain Carothers had
no way of knowing these things apart from the Spirit of God

giving the interpretation to his spiritual language.

After the service, people told Merlin he was accurate in his praying and wondered at how he knew those things. It was supernaturally imparted knowledge through the interpretation of his prayer language. Now there is revival in that Presbyterian Church!

4. PROPHECY

The interpretation to your spiritual language may give you some idea concerning the future. I knew when I'd be married before I knew who my wife would be. God revealed it to me through interpretation.

In the early 1960's, Oral Roberts stood on a vacant piece of land and began to pray in tongues. He waited quietly for a moment and the interpretation came: "NOW IS THE TIME TO BUILD A UNIVERSITY FOR GOD." Dr. Roberts had the dream of building a Christ-centered university several years prior to that time, but now the Holy Spirit said, "IT'S TIME!" Even though he only had $11.00, he could move ahead in this faith venture with great confidence and determination. He knew it was God's timing!

5. DOCTRINE

This is teaching. God can teach us things through interpretation. Sometimes while I'm preparing my Sunday morning messages, I'll need more information, so I'll pray in tongues, get real quiet and wait for God to teach me more on the subject at hand. He never lets me down.

A word of caution is in order here, however. Never take an interpretation on an equal par with the Scriptures. The Bible is God's main teaching tool. Interpretation of tongues is only to supplement, not to substitute! The greatest pray-ERs in history have been students of God's written Word.

God desires to open a whole new dimension of communication through the spiritual language and interpretation.

How do you do it?

1. Make sure you are a genuine born-again Christian. (John 3:3-5)

2. Be filled with the Holy Spirit. (Luke 11:13, Acts 10:45-46)

3. Practice speaking in your spiritual language as an act of your will. Paul said, "I WILL PRAY WITH THE SPIRIT." Don't wait for the Holy Spirit to do it for you.

4. After speaking in tongues for several minutes, get quiet before the Lord.

5. Ask the Lord for the interpretation. (1 Corinthians 14:13)

6. Wait for the interpretation. Don't try to force it. It will come as a flash of inspiration or an idea. It will seem to come from the inside of you (that's where the Holy Spirit lives).

7. Verbalize the interpretation.

Now, use your spiritual language and interpretation! Add this new dimension to your regular prayer-life!

Obstacles | 30 |

Prayer is an adventure! It is a calculated adventure. Many people view prayer as sort of a slot machine: *Sometimes it works, sometimes it doesn't*. But that's not true. The adventure of prayer works 100% of the time.

There are, however, some obstacles to a successful life of prayer. In this final chapter, we will take a look at twenty of the most common obstacles to successful praying.

A young man sat in a teaching session where I talked about *Enemies of Answered Prayer*. He listed all the *enemies* on paper and placed the notes in his Bible. Later he told me that every time he had a problem in prayer, he would review his notes, locate the problem, administer the proper solution, and once again his prayer-life would come alive!

You can do the same! Take notes. Study this chapter carefully! Learn the hindrances to POWER WITH GOD and avoid them. Here we go:

1. *LACK OF WORSHIP.* This is one of the greatest obstacles to successful prayer.

> [23] But the hour cometh, and now is, when the true worshippers shall worship the Father in spirit and in truth: for the Father seeketh such to worship him.

²⁴ God is a Spirit: and they that worship him must worship him in spirit and in truth. (John 4:23-24)

Now we know that God heareth not sinners: but if any be a worshipper of God, and doeth his will, him he heareth. (John 9:31)

Unsuccessful prayers are usually too long on request and too short on worship.

In baseball, a home run is wasted if you don't touch first base. Worship is first base in the believer's prayerlife. Praise, thank, and worship the Father in prayer. Use your own words or use your prayer language. Make up songs to the Lord. Tell Him that you're "crazy" about Him. LOVE Him. Learn the amazing secret of worship!

2. *LACK OF HONESTY AND SINCERITY.* Notice in John 4:23-24, it says to worship God in Spirit and in TRUTH. Be sure you are being totally honest with God. Don't try to soft-color your sins. Confess them. Be totally truthful with God about everything.

The greatest prayer warriors in history have been people who have taken off their masks and laid themselves open in sincerity and truth before God and before people.

Pastor, don't be a "holy, holy, holy" hypocrite in front of your congregation. Let them know that you have failures too. I know of one congregation that grew tremendously, both spiritually and numerically, when the pastor told how he was tempted to steal a small item from a motel room. At first they were shocked, but the pastor's honesty gained him the respect of his congregation when he willingly admitted he was not "above" temptation.

Sincerity and honesty both before God and man are essential to an effective, successful prayerlife.

3. *SELF-PITY.* This is what I call "the poor-old-me" attitude. People with this attitude cannot receive answers to prayer because their focus is always on themselves instead of on God.

All of us have had occasional "pity parties," but what I'm referring to is habitual self-pity. Feeling sorry for yourself usually occurs when you look at a situation from the wrong angle. For example, a person may feel sorry for himself when he discovers that the chemical worth of his entire body is only about 92¢. It's true! You are made with about 92¢ worth of material. Poor old you! If you dwelt on this you might get depressed. But there is another angle.

The atoms in a human body have the potential energy of producing 11,400,000 kilowatt hours per pound! At the price of electricity today, that would mean you are worth about $600,000,000.00 per pound. I weigh about 190 pounds. That means, I'm physically worth $144,000,000,000.00. I'm a millionaire 114,000 times over!

Look at every adverse situation and understand that there is another way to view it. Blessings do sometimes come in disguised packages. Don't let the "poor-old-me" attitude rob you of power with God.

4. *USING THE WRONG RULES.* There are different rules for different types of prayer. You don't use the same rules for peititionary prayer that you do for intercessory prayer. In sports there are different games. For example, there is basketball, baseball, football, tennis, tether ball, golf, and soccer. All

these games use a ball, but there are different rules for playing each game. You can't expect to be successful in football using baseball rules.

Different types of prayers use different rules and principles, too. For example:

• *PETITIONARY PRAYER* — Make sure you have a Scripture which promises the answer. Pray once, thank God for the answer. No need to continue begging God if it's promised. To continue begging would be an insult to God.

• *SUPPLICATORY PRAYER* — This is the kind of prayer where you constantly pray over and over again, calling forth God's will until it arrives.

• *PRAYER OF FAITH* — This involves not only asking God, but also making a FAITH COMMAND to the situation.

• *INTERCESSORY PRAYER* — Continual prayer on behalf of others.

• *PRAYER OF COMMITMENT* — When you are unsure of God's will, you simply make your request known, but commit the right decision into the hands of the Lord.

I would suggest that you get all the information on prayer that you can. Study it! Learn it! Apply your knowledge.

5. *UNCONFESSED SIN.*

> If I regard iniquity in my heart, the Lord will not hear me. (Psalm 66;18)

> If we confess our sins, he is faithful and just to forgive us our sins, and to cleanse us from all unrighteousness. (1 John 1:9)

Notice: Only confessed sin receives forgiveness. The Blood of Jesus does not cleanse excuses.

6. *CAUSING DISCORD IN THE CHURCH.* (Read 2 Timothy 2:24-26; James 3:16 and Proverbs 6:16-19.) This person is a friend of the devil although he may not realize it.

7. *PRAYING TO BE SEEN OF MEN.* (Read Matthew 6:5-6.)

8. *EATING TOO MUCH PRIOR TO PRAYER.* This will cause your mind to wander and often you will feel too tired to pray.

9. *FEAR OF ASKING.* We are sometimes afraid to ask God for things if we think our request is "too big" or "too much" to ask. This is a trick of the devil. All through the Bible, God encourages His people to ASK!

10. *NOT WILLING TO PAY THE PRICE OF SUCCESSFUL PRAYER.* Prayer requires time. Prayer requires a whole-hearted decision to commit to its ministry. If you want to be a success at your work and calling, you must pay the price of praying.

11. *NOT LETTING THE WORD OF GOD ABIDE IN YOU.* The greatest prayer warriors in history have been students of the Word. (John 15:7; Matthew 4:4)

12. *UNFORGIVENESS.* (Mark 11: 23-26)

13. *WORRY.*

14. *OTHER PEOPLE'S FREE WILL.* God can cause certain circumstances to come about which will be conducive for a person to decide in favor of God's will, but He will never violate their right to choose.

To illustrate this point, I'll share a true story with you about a young Christian man whose wife ran off and left him. He listened to all the faith teachers at a special Christian camp meeting and picked up some good principles, but made a wrong application of them. He began making his faith confession, "My wife will be coming back to me." He confessed this to all his friends and family members. He was persistent. But one day, his former wife married another man and his faith was shattered.

You see, God will not violate another human being's free will. The young man was using the wrong application of a spiritual principle. He should have been interceding, pleading with God, that the desire of his ex-wife's heart would change. But even then, God wouldn't force her or any other person to make right decisions.

15. *LACK OF AGGRESSIVENESS.*

> From the days of John the Baptist until now, the kingdom of heaven has been forcefully advancing and forceful men lay hold of it. (Matthew 11:12 NIV)

God is no man's slave. Some people tell God to do this and do that as if He were some kind of employee. I have heard others commanding God to do things for them, "or else ...." That is not what I'm talking about when I say aggressiveness.

Aggressiveness means to go after something, even if it means going out on a limb. The limb is where the fruit is! Aggressiveness involves a faith risk. If you study the great fortunes of our day, you'll discover that most of them involved risks.

Jesus said, "Launch out into the deep." Don't play around the edges. Get aggressive in your prayer warfare.

16. *FAILING TO CAST DOWN IMAGINATIONS.*

Casting down imaginations, and every high thing that exalteth itself against the knowledge of God, and bringing into captivity every thought to the obedience of Christ. (2 Corinthians 10:5)

Your imagination can be a help or a hindrance to your prayer-life. Stop and think, what do you picture? Victory or defeat? Health or sickness? Prosperity or poverty? Get your imagination to work for you instead of against you. Picture yourself in possession of that which you requested of God!

17. *ALLOWING YOUR FEELINGS TO RULE.* There are times when we don't sense God's presence, power, or love, but must accept it by faith because He said He'd never leave us. He said that He loves us with an everlasting love. We must believe that.

We all go through undulations. There seems to be a universal law stating that we'll have high peaks and low points in our lives. Sometimes we *feel* saved, sometimes we don't. Sometimes we *feel* like praying, sometimes we don't. Mature Christians have learned to do the right thing because it is right, not because of feelings.

One year after John Wesley (the great Methodist preacher) became a Christian, he wrote, "I know that I am not a Christian. I know it because I do not feel that I love God and His son Jesus Christ...." Thank God, Wesley eventually learned that we are saved NOT because we feel like it, but because God said it.

God did not say, "Ask, if you feel like it." (Luke 11:9) Don't let feelings or lack of feelings hinder your prayer life.

18. *A SPIRIT OF HURRY.*

> Be still and know that I am God: I will be exalted among the heathen, I will be exalted in the earth. (Psalm 46:10)

19. *IMPATIENCE.* Answered prayer comes to us from heaven at different speeds. God sends the answers the very moment we pray in faith, however, our maturity and the intents of our heart, will determine the speed at which the answer travels.

When I was in the Navy, there were certain places the ship could not go unless the tide was in. If the captain tried to guide the ship into a channel that was too shallow, the bottom may get stuck. So the ship and all the passengers had to wait out at sea until the tide came in and the channel's water rose to a non-dangerous level for heavy ship traffic. It didn't matter if everyone aboard griped and complained and hollered that they wanted to go ashore. The captain knew better than to pull the ship into port before the water level permitted.

Our captain (JESUS) knows when the "tide is in," and when the answer should arrive. Trust Him!

20. *FAILING TO EXPECT THE ANSWER.*

When you pray in faith you must fully expect God to answer.

CONCLUSION

You can eliminate these twenty prayer obstacles and turn your prayer-life into an affair of excitement, adventure, and POWER WITH GOD. But remember, a home run doesn't count unless you go by first base. Worship is "first base" in the prayer-life of the believer. Head for first base first.

And don't forget this either: You can run to first base only if you're a member of the team. You become a member of the team by asking Jesus Christ to be your Captain!

HOW TO MAKE JESUS THE "CAPTAIN" OF YOUR LIFE:

1.   ACKNOWLEDGE: "For all have sinned and come short of the glory of God." (Romans 3:23) "God be merciful to me a sinner." (Luke 18:13) You must acknowledge in the light of God's Word that you are a sinner.

2.   REPENT: "Except ye repent, ye shall all likewise perish." (Luke 13:3) "Repent ye therefore, and be converted that your sins may be blotted out." (Acts 3:19) You must see the awfulness of sin and then repent of it.

3.   CONFESS: "If we confess our sins, he is faithful and just to forgive us our sins, and to cleanse us from all unrighteousness." (1 John 1:9) "With the mouth confession is made unto salvation." (Romans 10:10) Confess not to men but to God.

4. FORSAKE: "Let the wicked forsake his way, and the unrighteous man his thoughts: and let him return unto the Lord...for he will abundantly pardon." (Isaiah 55:7) Sorrow for sin is not enough in itself. We must want to be done with it once and for all.

5. BELIEVE: "For God so loved the world, that he gave his only begotten Son, that whosoever believeth in him should not perish, but have everlasting life." (John 3:16) "If thou shalt confess with thy mouth the Lord Jesus, and shalt believe in thine heart that God hath raised him from the dead, thou shalt

be saved." (Romans 10:9) Believe in the finished work of Christ on the cross.

6. RECEIVE: "He came unto his own, and his own received him not. But as many as received him, to them gave he power to become the sons of God, even to them that believe on his name." (John 1:11,12) You must personally receive Christ into your heart by faith, if the experience of the New Birth is to be yours (FGBMFI).

ABOUT THE AUTHOR

Dave Williams has been pastor of Mount Hope Church and International Outreach Ministries since 1980. On the ministry's scenic 43 acres sits the multi-million dollar worship and teaching center designed to comfortably seat over 3000 people. The new complex includes educational facilities, executive offices, a television production center, and world outreach headquarters.

Williams is the founder and president of Mount Hope Bible Training Institute. The accredited Institute equips men and women for the work of the ministry, both lay and full time.

Author of 96 audio cassette teaching programs and two leadership video training programs, Dave Williams has also written 34 books, including the international seven-time best seller, *A New Life ... The Start of Something Wonderful*, now in its 11th printing. His written articles and reviews have appeared in newspapers and magazines nationwide, including *Advance*, *Ministries Today*, and *The Pentecostal Evangel*.

The weekly telecast, *DAVE WILLIAMS AND THE PACESETTER'S PATH*, is heard over a variety of radio stations. His international speaking ministry has taken him to several nations including Europe, Tanzania, South Africa, Latin America, and other places of the world.

In September of 1987, Pastor Williams was presented the "Key to the City" by Lansing Mayor Terry McKane. He was also honored by the Michigan State Legislature in 1988 for his contribution to the spiritual enrichment of the state of Michigan. He serves as an executive presbyter for The Assemblies of God-Michigan District, and is a past regent for North Central Bible College in Minneapolis. He currently serves as a board member for The Assemblies of God Division of Foreign Missions.

The 42-year-old pastor resides in Grand Ledge, Michigan with his wife and two children. He is an ordained Assemblies of God minister.

For a complete catalog of books, tapes, videos, and courses by Dave Williams, write to: Dave Williams, 202 South Creyts Road, Lansing, MI 48917-9284

Please include your prayer requests and comments when you write.

FAITHBUILDING BOOKS
by Dave Williams

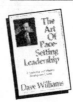

THE ART OF PACESETTING LEADERSHIP

Are you the kind of leader God is looking for? Find out by reading The Art of Pacesetting Leadership — an entire Leadership & Ministry Development course in itself. Taken from Pastor Dave's highly acclaimed "Pacesetting Leadership" class, this book's topics include: Levels of Leadership, Qualities Exhibited in Master-Level Leaders, The Kind of Leader God is Looking For, How to Overcome Stress and Pressure in the Ministry, and so much more. This is perhaps Pastor Williams' most important book.

0-938020-34-X $7.95

THE PASTOR'S PAY

Most church members have little or no knowledge of the concerns, frustrations, and needs of their pastor. Dave Williams, in a gentle, tender way, takes a close look at how much a pastor is worth, who sets his pay, and the scriptural guidelines for paying him. You'll learn the Biblical principles for setting the pastor's pay.

0-938020-36-6 .... $4.95

SLAIN IN THE SPIRIT IS IT REAL OR FAKE?

What would you think if you saw someone fall, as if dead, to the ground? What if the fall accompanied foaming at the mouth? . . . moaning and groaning? Is it real? Is it fake? This book explains Satanic Manifestations versus God's Visitations, The Supernatural Power and Manifestations of God's Glory, The Purpose of Signs and Wonders, Abuses and Shams, The History of This Phenomenon, Why Some Oppose This Manifestation, and When Does Being Slain in the Spirit Occur.

0-938020-32-3 .... $1.50

GETTING TO KNOW YOUR HEAVENLY FATHER

This book will lead you into that personal relationship with your heavenly Father you so desire. It discusses Christianity as a wonderful and fulfilling family relationship, not merely a religious experience. Find out the difference between theological tradition and the truth of God's character. Also included are Principles For Parents, and How to Claim Your Daily Benefits As a Child of God.

0-938020-35-8 .... $1.50

15 BIG CAUSES OF FAILURE

God did not create you to fail. He created you to succeed and have victory in every area of your life. This Mount Hope micro-book book takes a look at 15 common causes of failure in believer's lives and how to avoid them. You'll also learn how to get on that road to success which God has ordained for your life.

0-938020-13-7 .... $1.00

■ Quantity Discounts Available ■
MOUNT HOPE PUBLICATIONS
202 S. Creyts Rd. ■ Lansing, MI 48917

FAITHBUILDING BOOKS
by Dave Williams

THE AIDS PLAGUE

How does the AIDS crisis affect you? Believe it or not, before long everyone will be affected in some way or another by the tragedy of this deadly virus. Is there any hope? YES! In this book, Dave Williams gives you the answer to the AIDS crisis and tells how you can be protected.

0-938020-38-2 .... $1.95

END-TIMES BIBLE PROPHECY —
My Personal Sermon Notes

These are Dave Williams' actual sermon notes from an extended series on Bible prophecy. In a concise form, you can now study events that will affect you: The Rapture • The Great Tribulation • The Coming of Antichrist…and much more.

0-938020-39-0 .... $1.75

THE SUPERNATURAL GIFTS
OF THE HOLY SPIRIT — My Personal Sermon Notes

What a terrific reference resource. Students, teachers, preachers, anybody can benefit from these actual notes from Dave Williams' sermons on spiritual gifts. These compact, practical outlined notes on the Gifts of the Holy Spirit will help you to study like never before.

0-938020-40-4 .... $1.75

SUPERNATURAL SOULWINNING

Something big is happening! God has given us just a little more time to participate in His end-time revival. That means you and I have the chance to see this revival explode into the greatest, most successful harvest before the Church blasts off from this earth in a cloud of glory and splendor. How can we reach so many people if time is so short? How can we see our loved ones, our neighbors, our co-workers saved? These are questions Pastor Dave brought to the Lord in urgent prayer. In Supernatural Soulwinning, Dave Williams shares the simple plan God gave him for this enormous end-time revival.

0-938020-41-2 .... $1.95

SOMEBODY OUT THERE NEEDS YOU!

But I'm no evangelist," you say? That may be true. Your gift may not be that of an evangelist, but that doesn't exclude you from being a soulwinner. Along with salvation comes the great privilege of spreading the gospel. And that doesn't need to be burdensome; it's the mistakes we make while trying to witness that discourage us and make evangelism seem like a hard task. Learning how to avoid these 12 common mistakes will help you evangelize your friends, neighbors and loved ones.

0-938020-42-0 .... $1.75

• Quantity Discounts Available •
MOUNT HOPE PUBLICATIONS
202 S. Creyts Rd. • Lansing, MI 48917

FAITHBUILDING BOOKS
by Dave Williams

DECEPTION, DELUSION & DESTRUCTION

Someone wants desperately to deceive you . . . but you can crush any attempt toward your destruction. The Bible gives you clear-cut guidelines on how to recognize deception and keep free from all forms of spiritual blindness. Deception, Delusion & Destruction unmasks deception, reveals its most likely targets, and explains how you can recognize it in its most deadly form — religious deception.

0-938020-43-9 .... $4.95

FAITHBUILDING VIDEO MESSAGES
VHS by Dave Williams

PACESETTING LEADERSHIP

Pastor Dave's highly acclaimed "Pacesetting Leadership" class on video. Topics include: Levels of Leadership, Qualities Exhibited in Master-Level Leaders, The Kind of Leader God is Looking For, How to Overcome Stress and Pressure in the Ministry, and *so much more.*

14 Sessions $239.70

MINISTRY GROWTH AND SUCCESS

Dave Williams' Advanced Leadership Course on video. You'll learn: How to Lead So People See It's God • How to Minister the Holy Spirit Baptism • Church Diseases & Cures • How to Motivate People • Getting Things Done • Writing as a Ministry

10 Sessions $171.25

WHAT TO DO WHEN YOU'VE
LOST YOUR MOTIVATION

• The Importance of Motivation • What Happens When We Lose Our Motivation • What Causes a Loss of Motivation • How To Revive Your Motivation

2 Hour Video $19.95

■ Quantity Discounts Available ■
MOUNT HOPE PUBLICATIONS
202 S. Creyts Rd. ■ Lansing, MI 48917

FAITHBUILDING VIDEO MESSAGES

V H S by Dave Williams

THE PASTOR'S PAY

A motivational one-hour video featuring Dave Williams speaking about the minister's pay. This video will motivate pastors and board members to study, in depth, how God feels about the pastor's pay.

1 Hour Video $12.95

THE UNPARDONABLE SIN
AND THE SIN UNTO DEATH

• Confusion Over the "Unpardonable Sin" • How Can We Understand the Unpardonable Sin • 5 Phases to Committing the Unpardonable Sin • 2 Types of Death • 3 Keys to a Longer Life • Some Who Came Under the Sin Unto Death • Some Who Repented in Time

2 Hour Video $19.95

YOUR GREATEST WEAPON
IN THE STORMS OF LIFE

• A Great Lesson In Faith • The Power of Life is in the Tongue • The Kind of Words Jesus Spoke • How to Speak the Results You Want • Faith Words — Your Greatest Weapon Against the Storms of Life

2 Hour Video $19.95

10 COMMANDMENTS
FOR GUARANTEED FAILURE

• Success or Failure . . . The Choice Is Yours
• 10 Commandments Guaranteed to Make You a Successful Failure . . . OR
• Don't Do These and You'll Succeed

1 Hour Video $12.95

For your convenience, you may order any product listed here by using the form on the following pages.

• Quantity Discounts Available •
MOUNT HOPE PUBLICATIONS
202 S. Creyts Rd. ▪ Lansing, MI 48917

FAITHBUILDING PRODUCTS
for Pacesetting People by Dave Williams

ORDER FORM

Qty.	Title	Price	Amt.
BOOKS			
____	The A.I.D.S. Plague	1.95	_____
____	Deception, Delusion & Destruction	4.95	_____
____	Supernatural Soulwinning	1.95	_____
____	Somebody Out There Needs You!	1.75	_____
____	End Time Bible Prophecy (Study Notes)	1.75	_____
____	Supernatural Gifts of the Holy Spirit (Study Notes)	1.75	_____
____	The Secret of Power With God	7.95	_____
____	The Christian Job-Hunter's Handbook	3.25	_____
____	The NEW LIFE: The Start of Something Wonderful	1.95	_____
____	The NEW LIFE (Spanish Edition)	1.95	_____
____	Setting & Reaching Your Faith Goals	3.95	_____
____	Genuine Prosperity: A Biblical Perspective	1.25	_____
____	How to Get Out of the Tormenting Cave of Depression	1.50	_____
____	Growing Up in Our Father's Family	1.25	_____
____	You Can Win With Patient Determination (microbook)	1.00	_____
____	The Beauty of Holiness	1.25	_____
____	The Grand Finale: A Study on the Coming End-Time Revival	1.75	_____
____	The Ministry of the Laying On of Hands	1.75	_____
____	Lonely in the Midst of a Crowd	1.25	_____
____	Understanding Spiritual Gifts	1.75	_____
____	The Desires of Your Heart Can Become Realities	2.95	_____
____	Remedy for Worry & Tension	1.25	_____
____	7 Signposts on the Road to Spiritual Maturity	1.50	_____
____	Getting to Know Your Heavenly Father	1.50	_____
____	Revival Power of Music (microbook)	1.00	_____
____	Slain in the Spirit: Is It Real or Fake?	1.50	_____
____	Finding Your Ministry & Gifts	5.95	_____
____	The Art of Pacesetting Leadership	7.95	_____
____	The Pastor's Pay	4.95	_____
____	Tongues and Interpretation (microbook)	1.00	_____
____	15 Big Causes of Failure (microbook)	1.00	_____
____	How to Invest An Hour in Prayer	1.75	_____
____	Success Principles from the Lips of Jesus	2.95	_____
COURSES			
____	The Art of Pacesetting Leadership	69.95	_____
____	Ministry Growth & Development	59.95	_____
____	Your Financial Success	37.95	_____
____	Supernatural Gifts of the Spirit	37.95	_____
____	Successful Church Governments	59.95	_____

AUDIO CASSETTE SETS

____ The Pastor's Pay (2 cassettes)	10.00	_____
____ Relief from Worry & Pressures (3 cassettes)	15.00	_____
____ Spiritual Warfare (12 cassettes)	50.00	_____
____ Fasting for the Impossible (2 cassettes)	10.00	_____
____ The Coming "Grand Finale" Revival (4 cassettes)	20.00	_____
____ The Supernatural Gifts (4 cassettes)	20.00	_____
____ Your Greatest Weapons in the Storms of Life (2 cassettes)	10.00	_____
____ Intercessory Prayer (3 cassettes)	15.00	_____
____ What To Do When You've Lost Your Motivation (2 csts)	10.00	_____
____ End-Times Bible Prophecy (3 cassettes)	15.00	_____

VIDEOS

____ 10 Commandments for Failure	12.95	_____
____ Your Greatest Weapon in the Storms of Life	19.95	_____
____ What To Do When You've Lost Your Motivation	19.95	_____
____ The Art of Pacesetting Leadership (14 sessions)	239.70	_____
____ Ministry Growth & Development (10 sessions)	171.25	_____
____ The Pastor's Pay (1 session)	12.95	_____

TOTAL ORDER $ _____

Please include Payment with Order. Thank You!

DISCOUNT & QUANTITY PRICES: Discount and quantity prices are available for ministers, churches, non-profit organizations, and book stores. Please write to DAVCO COMMUNICATIONS, P.O. Box 80386, Lansing, MI 48917-0386 or telephone (517) 321-2780.

INDIVIDUAL ORDERS: For individual orders, please write to: THE HOPE STORE, 202 S. Creyts Road, Lansing, MI 48917. Tel: (517) 321-2780

Michigan Residents: Please include appropriate sales tax.

Orders are processed immediately upon receipt. Please include full payment with your order. It helps us to serve you better, avoiding C.O.D.s and billings. VISA and MasterCard orders accepted.

PLEASE PRINT CLEARLY

Name _____

Address _____

City _____

State _____ ZIP _____

Please include $1.50 for postage and handling on all orders less than $20.00. Thanks!

VISA ____   MasterCard ____

Expiration Date _____

Signature _____